A VERY FAR PLACE

Tales of Tawi-Tawi

H. ARLO NIMMO

ATENEO DE MANILA UNIVERSITY PRESS

140580

ATENEO DE MANILA UNIVERSITY PRESS
Bellarmine Hall, Katipunan Avenue
Loyola Heights, Quezon City
P.O. Box 154, 1099 Manila, Philippines
Tel.: (632) 426-59-84 / Fax (632) 426-59-09
E-mail: unipress@admu.edu.ph
Website: www.ateneopress.org

Copyright 2012 by Ateneo de Manila University
and H. Arlo Nimmo

Book and cover design by Karl Fredrick M. Castro

The National Library of the Philippines CIP Data

    Recommended entry:

    Nimmo, H. Arlo.
        A very far place : tales of Tawi-Tawi / H. Arlo
    Nimmo. -- Quezon city : Ateneo de Manila
    University Press, 2012.
            p. ; cm.

    ISBN 978-971-550-657-1

        1. Anthropologists--Fiction. 2. Tawi-Tawi
    (Philippines)--Social life and customs--Fiction
    3. Sama Dilaut (Philippine people)--Social life and
    customs--Fiction.   I. Title.

    PR9550.9   899.2103083   2012   P220121201

To

Tarabasa Idji and Antonio Alari

who introduced me to the beautiful island world

of Tawi-Tawi.

Contents

Tawi-Tawi,

a very far place,

a flooded place filled with islands.

SAMA DILAUT WIND SONG

A VERY FAR PLACE

Mindanao Studies
Antonio de Castro, Series Editor

The Mindanao Studies Series published by the Ateneo de Manila University Press seeks to make available to the public works on Mindanao, its peoples, languages, histories, and cultures. In doing so, the series also wishes to promote a "Mindanao consciousness" among the peoples of the southern islands, i.e., a consciousness that graciously respects and creatively expresses the irreducible richness and interconnected particularities of Mindanao and its inhabitants.

Featuring scholarly works based on primary and secondary research materials, including academic essays across the disciplines, the series serves as a multidisciplinary forum for communicating new information, new interpretations, and recent research concerning Mindanao. The series is also open to the publication of works that express the artistic sensibility and literary creativity of its peoples.

Tawi-Tawi

For two years in the mid-1960s, I conducted anthropological research in the Tawi-Tawi Islands at the end of the Sulu Archipelago in the southern Philippines among the Sama Dilaut, a nomadic boat-dwelling people also known as the Bajau.

Tawi-Tawi is the southernmost province in the Philippines, a collection of over one hundred islands, all small and many tiny, situated a few nautical miles east of Borneo across the Sulawesi Sea from Indonesia. A few degrees above the equator, the province is culturally more Indonesian than Filipino because of its proximity to that country and a shared Muslim religion. The islands were inhabited by two groups of Sama people: the Sama Dilaut ("Sea Sama") lived on the sea in small houseboats and the Sama Dea ("Land Sama") in coastal villages in pile houses. A few Tausug people from the northern Sulu Islands were found in some of the Land Sama villages. Chinese traders and shop-keepers were scattered throughout the islands, but most were concentrated in the port towns of Bongao and Sitangkai as was the little Christian Filipino community consisting of mostly government bureaucrats and members of the Philippine militia.

The small population of Sama Dilaut moved among five moorages fishing and collecting from Tawi-Tawi's great sprawling reefs. They traded their surpluses to the Land Sama for fruits and vegetables, and what remained was sold to fish buyers in Bongao, the capital of the islands. Their houseboats typically housed a single nuclear family, but occasionally another related family or elderly parents shared the boat. The Land Sama were Muslims, but most Sama Dilaut retained their indigenous religion which was directed to the appeasement of ancestral and other spirits. A large population of Sama Dilaut lived further down the archipelago at Sitangkai Island where they had moved to houses and were rapidly becoming incorporated into Islam. The main focus of my research explored the socio-cultural changes that occurred as the boat-dwelling Sama Dilaut became house-dwellers.

The Philippine Air Force maintained a skeletal outpost on Sanga-Sanga Island where commercial flights of Philippine Air Lines were scheduled to arrive twice weekly but often did not. The Air Force base had a jeep as did the small Philippine Navy base on Tawi-Tawi Island; the only other vehicle in the islands was an engine-less truck in the port town of Bongao that was occasionally pushed from the wharf up and down the town's only street delivering and picking up goods. Three Chinese-owned cargo ships from Zamboanga regularly navigated the

Sulu Archipelago with ports-of-call at Jolo, Siasi, Bongao, and Sitangkai carrying passengers, depositing materiel and picking up copra and dried fish. Motorized launches transported people and goods throughout the islands, but many islanders still relied on sailboats for their travels.

The islands were beautiful as only tropical islands can be. Palm-covered coral islands and multicolored reefs flanked the southern shores of the long, mountainous island of Tawi-Tawi that gave the archipelago its name. Villages of pile houses, nestled in shallow shore waters, occasionally interrupted the symmetry of the white sand beaches. Bongao Island with its legendary peak and perhaps three thousand residents served as capital and port of the islands. Its unpaved street wandered from the wharf along the edge of the little town until it dissipated into a path that meandered around the island through small seaside villages, each with a rustic mosque that called its faithful to prayer every morning and evening.

I was a young American Ph.D. candidate in anthropology exploring a very alien culture while getting my feet wet in the adult business of living. My job was to describe the Sama Dilaut socio-cultural system for the world of anthropology and anyone else who might be interested. It hadn't been documented by anthropologists or anyone else except a few passing travelers who left mostly superficial, misleading accounts.

Sometimes it seemed I was living at the edge of the earth, back of the back of beyond. Most of the islands were remote in those days before the technological revolution of recent years that has interconnected the globe. Eons separated me from the Sama Dilaut. I was from the industrial West, the nuclear age, the age of space, but I was living not too differently from the way much of the world lived centuries ago. As I learned the language of the Sama Dilaut and participated in their lives, I ceased being a stranger from another world and probably became as much a Sama Dilaut as is possible for an outsider.

I left Tawi-Tawi a very different man from the one who arrived. Few things frightened me anymore and even fewer intimidated me. I watched babies born and sometimes saw them die. I helped dig graves and lower corpses into them. I encountered an ancient spirit world through the guidance and rituals of shamans. I joined fishermen in their myriad methods of harvesting the rich marine life of the reefs and open sea. I learned the cycles of the sea and after almost drowning came to respect its unpredictable moods. I spent long, sometimes lonely nights gazing at star-filled skies, accepting my flaws and discovering my merits. I lived life at its most elemental and would forever see the world through different lenses.

This book of stories was inspired by those experiences. It is part memoir, part ethnography but mostly fiction. The stories are true to the culture and geography of Tawi-Tawi in the 1960s although some place names are fictitious. The characters and events are entirely fictitious, the creations of my imagination.

Sitangkai Overnight

cross the dark reef, the lights of the *Zamboanga Star* illuminated the distant wharf. The ship arrived in late afternoon, but the small boats that transported its cargo over the reef to and from Sitangkai had awaited the high tide so they could move above the reef rather than wend through its serpentine low tide channels. The night was warm and dark with a cloud-cover hiding the trillions of stars overhead. I waited until after dinner, a rather grand name for my modest meal of fish and cassava, before hitching a ride to the wharf with Nuni, one of the stevedores who transported crates of dried fish to the ship and returned with rice, Cokes and other materiel for the shelves of Sitangkai's Chinese merchants.

The night was quiet. Nuni and his brother respected the silence, saying nothing while poling their heavy cargo through the shallow black waters. Only the gentle swish of their poles moving in and out of the water interrupted the quietude. Behind us, the lights of Sitangkai grew dimmer as we moved away from the little floating town called "the Venice of the

Philippines" by tourism promoters in Manila. The wharf emerged from the sea two miles away on a tiny manmade islet at the edge of a sprawling coral reef that inhibited the further approach of sea-going ships. As we neared the wharf, the ship's bright lights provided an island of harsh illumination and its generators and stevedores added noise to the night. Nuni and his brother switched from poles to paddles when we reached the deep waters. They jumped to the wharf and secured the boat. I followed with my duffle bag.

I'd been in Sitangkai for three months of fieldwork among the Sama Dilaut who resided in the little town at the very end of the Philippines, a stone's throw from Borneo. I was on my way out for a break, not entirely a vacation since I was committed to an anthropology conference in Zamboanga. But after the conference, I would fly to Manila for whatever pleasures I might find there.

About a dozen Sama Dilaut boats clustered around the wharf where the ship's cargo was stacked. The *Zamboanga Star*, an old World War II mine sweeper converted to commercial use, was one of three Chinese-owned cargo ships that routinely made the tediously slow roundtrip trek from Zamboanga to Sitangkai. The men unloaded their crates of dried fish into the ship's hold and then filled their boats with the ship's cargo for transport over the reef to Sitangkai. Everything was loaded and unloaded manually, automation belonged to another world. The back-breaking labor usually took all night. When the ship was loaded, it sounded its horn in tired farewell and the exhausted stevedores returned to Sitangkai to sleep away the day.

Two Chinese men from the ship directed the stevedores. I approached one I knew from previous trips.

"Hi Leung," I said. "A long time since I've seen you."

"Yes, my friend," he said, obviously having forgotten my name. "Will you be traveling with us?"

"Yes. Do you have a cabin?" The ship's eight grubby little cabins accommodated the more affluent passengers. Most local travelers occupied the rows of army cots that stretched over the deck. I'd spent many a restless night on the hard cots, within inches of sleeping neighbors with their penned chickens, bundles of dried fish, and sometimes crying babies. I hoped a cabin was available. Its bed wouldn't be any more comfortable than those on deck, but it would provide some privacy.

"You're in luck," said Leung. "I think two cabins are still available. Go aboard and one of the boys will take care of you."

"Thanks. Any idea when we might leave?" I asked, making conversation since I knew from experience that too many variables made departure time unpredictable.

"Hopefully at dawn. Before the tide goes out."

I approached the gangplank, but stepped aside to make room for two young men bent with heavy bags of rice on their backs. I recognized them and they smiled at my greeting.

On deck I found a crewman and told him Leung said cabins were available. He looked me over, said nothing, and motioned me to follow him. We twisted through the crowded deck, stepping around and over cargo and passengers. We reached the cabins in the center, four on either side, back to back. My guide opened a door on the port side and invited me to check out the facilities. It was tiny with only a cot and enough space to turn around. A small window beside the door was glassless. The sheet on the cot and the lumpy pillow had obviously accommodated another passenger, probably several. I asked to see the other cabin and was led to starboard. He opened a door and I stepped inside the equally small, equally grungy, and equally slept-in cabin. It, too, had a glassless window. This side of the ship was less active so I told him I'd take the cabin. I gave him an expected tip and he left. I squeezed into the tiny room. I turned the pillow case inside-out thinking the inside might be cleaner, but someone had beat me to it. I turned the sheet over and discovered several people had slept on that side too. I closed the door and lay on my back enjoying the first privacy I'd had in many days.

I fell asleep but was almost immediately awakened by stevedores shouting outside my cabin. I didn't feel like joining the fracas so I lay and watched the cockroaches dart across the peeling paint on the grimy ceiling. But the stuffy cabin and its stale smells eventually coaxed me outside. I leaned on a rail and watched the activity on the wharf below. The ship's lights illuminated the sweating bodies of the stevedores, stripped to shorts and loincloths, as they moved in and out of the darkness. Occasionally one jumped into the sea for some cool respite, shook himself dry, and rejoined his companions. Always the anthropologist, I jotted down names of men I recognized, noting who was working with whom, to document the social organization of their work.

Behind me, four Chinese men, fish buyers who traveled with the ship and bought dried fish at the ports-of-call, sat at a small table playing mahjong. Their game was wordless but the slap of the tiles on the tabletop added staccato sounds to the rhythm of the night. I checked out the passengers on the cots scattered over the deck. A few were traveling alone, but most had companions, almost certainly kinsmen. An old woman beside me cradled a small girl in her lap as she blankly watched the activities, periodically leaning over the rail to emit a mouthful of red betel juice into the sea. A man on my right lay on his cot with three immobilized chickens. An old man four cots away read from his *Koran*. An occasional baby cried, but most children were sleeping. I looked at my watch. It was 11:30. Six more hours until dawn and the ship's departure.

I was becoming bored. The light was too dim for reading and I didn't feel like returning to my stuffy cabin so I decided

to explore the deck. I crossed to port where I was surprised
to see a Caucasian woman leaning against the rail, smoking
a cigarette and watching the stevedores on the wharf below.
She wore dark wrap-around sunglasses, white shorts, a red
halter, and rubber flip-flops. Blond and pale, she had obviously
shunned the sun. She glanced at me and quickly turned away.
Undaunted, I approached her.

"Good evening," I said, leaning on the rail beside her.
"Looks like we have a few more hours before the ship leaves."

"Yes, it appears that way," she said in American English,
watching the activity below and not looking at me.

"Have you been visiting Sitangkai?" I asked, knowing
she hadn't. News of her appearance would have reached me
immediately in the little town.

"No. I haven't left the ship. I'm touring the islands." She
turned and the light illuminated her face. She wore heavy
makeup and was older than I initially thought, perhaps forty.
Her full bosom spilled from her halter.

"Beautiful islands, aren't they?" I said.

"Yes, they are." She paused. "Are you a tourist too?"

"No. I'm an anthropologist. I'm doing research in
Sitangkai."

"Oh, how interesting," she said blandly. She obviously didn't
think it was the least bit interesting.

"Are you traveling alone?"

"Yes."

She offered no more, but I persevered. "What brings a lone American woman to the end of the Philippines?"

"Curiosity, perhaps. And a time to be alone. Time to think through some things."

"We all need occasional time-outs."

She didn't respond and continued watching the activities below.

"I know," she finally said. She flipped her cigarette over the side. It hit the water with a sharp hiss. "Sometimes we get caught up in relationships that turn out different from what we planned. But we grow and change over the years and they're not the same."

"I take it you're reconsidering a relationship."

"Yes. One I entered when I was very young and never really understood. Now I'm beginning to understand what I got myself into. Or trying to."

"A marriage?"

"Something like that." She smiled to herself and said, "How about you? What are you doing way down here all by yourself?"

"Like I said, I'm an anthropologist."

"I know, but what's behind the anthropologist? There has to be more. Why here? Why anthropology?"

I laughed. "Wait a minute. I'm the anthropologist. I'm supposed to be asking the questions." I paused. "But if you have a spare month I'll tell you all about it."

"Seriously. What brought you to anthropology and one of the most remote places in the Philippines?"

"Like you, some of it was curiosity. But I guess mostly to learn more about myself. Trying to figure out my place in the scheme of things. I never felt in synch with my own culture. Maybe I'm trying to find one where I fit better."

"Maybe that's what life's about. Trying to find a place where we fit. And when we think we've found it, periodically reviewing it to see if we're still in that place. Or if we should move on." She laughed. "How did we get into this heavy discussion?"

"My fault," I said. "I posed the philosophical question of 'Good evening.'"

She laughed again and pulled a cigarette from a pack in her pocket and lit it. She offered one to me. I declined and noticed that her little finger was missing. She saw me looking at her hand and wiggled both hands at me. The little fingers of each hand were missing. "You've heard of 'six-fingered people'? I belong to the four-fingered clan."

"I'm sorry," I said, embarrassed. "I didn't mean to stare."

"I'm used to it."

"What kind of work do you do when you're not traveling in Asia?" I asked, changing the subject. A loud thud startled me and I turned to see a burly Sama Dilaut youth wearing only a loincloth standing beside the crate he'd dropped, his bare body glistening and his eyes devouring the woman beside me. She returned his look. He picked up his crate and stacked it with others at the stern.

She remembered my question. "I have an . . . office job. Secretarial work. With a company in Chicago."

For some reason I didn't believe her.

"I bet you're happy to be away from the Chicago winter."

"Yes, I am." She stood aside to allow the passage of two men struggling with oversized crates of dried fish. "I think I'll go to my cabin. I'm tired. It was nice talking with you."

"And with you. Perhaps I'll see you in the morning."

"Yes. Perhaps." She walked through the cluttered deck and disappeared on the other side of the ship.

I continued watching the stevedores, wondering if I was sleepy enough to confront my cabin. Leung, who was directing the deck activities, approached and stood beside me. "Are you leaving Sitangkai?" he asked.

"Only for a couple of weeks. I'm stopping in Bongao for a few days. Then I'm going to Zamboanga and Manila."

"Do you know that woman you were talking to?"

"No, I just met her. Do you?"

"No. She's been on the ship since Zamboanga. She's a tourist." He paused. "I don't think she's a good woman."

He left without further explanation. I assumed her brief attire triggered his assessment. I watched the stevedores a while longer and decided to face my cabin for whatever sleep I might squeeze from the night.

I wrapped a T-shirt around the grubby pillow and lay on the paper-thin mattress wishing I'd taken one of the cots on the deck which were noisier but cooler. My only light came from the weak rays that filtered through my glassless window. An occasional head passed the window, but otherwise I was undisturbed. The outside noises subsided into a muted, comfortable cacophony and I fell asleep.

About an hour later, a loud thud against the wall jolted me awake. I looked at my watch. It was one o'clock. I stared into the darkness. Sounds outside told me the ship was still loading. I heard another thud on the wall followed by the unmistakable rhythms and murmurs of fornication. "I hope they keep it short," I muttered and rolled over to a more comfortable position. A slammed door climaxed the noises next door.

I sighed in relief and prepared for more sleep. Such was not to be. In the cabin beside me, a door opened and closed, and moments later the cot squeakily sagged with the weight of an additional body. Thumps hit my wall and again the sounds of sex filtered through. Minutes later they ceased, the cot groaned, and the door slammed. Hopefully that was the end of it. I slipped into sleep.

A muffled cry startled me awake yet again. The wall shook with renewed activity. By this time, I was both irritated and curious about what was going on and decided to investigate. I opened the door and stepped onto the deck. The air was heavy and humid but cooler than my cabin. Most of the people on the cots were sleeping except two old men who quietly discussed something that seemed very serious. The stevedores were still loading the ship. I walked to the port side, skirting stacks of cargo. A stevedore was leaning against the rail. He saw me and quickly looked the other direction where another stevedore was leaving a cabin. He approached the waiting man, whispered to him, and walked past me with a big smile. The waiting stevedore disappeared into the cabin. A young man I recognized from Sitangkai approached me, smiled and said, "Are you waiting?"

"Waiting for what?"

"The woman," he said, nodding toward the cabin. "She's free."

"What are you talking about?"

"The American woman. Everyone's doing her. Are you waiting for her?"

Prostitutes occasionally traveled up and down the archipelago on the cargo ships, stopping a few days in the port towns. I knew they occasionally tricked with the horny male crews, but the American woman obviously wasn't in it for the money.

"No, I'm not waiting," I said.

"You can go ahead of me," he offered generously.

"No thanks."

The man emerged from the active cabin, looking somewhat sheepish, and passed us saying nothing.

"I will go now," said my companion.

"Enjoy."

I returned to starboard and watched the ongoing loading of the ship. I glanced at my watch. Three o'clock. I was sleepy and decided to return to my stuffy cabin. I considered stripping to my briefs, but changed my mind when I saw the grimy sheet. I lay down. The cabin beside me was quiet. Maybe she was satiated for the night, or perhaps she'd exhausted all the interested men onboard. I drifted to sleep and didn't wake until dawn when the ship's horn announced its departure. In distant Sitangkai, I heard the morning call to prayer. I rolled over and returned to sleep.

Sunshine was pouring through my little window when I awakened. The cabin was stifling and I was wet with sweat. I went onto the deck hoping to find a breeze, but found none. I descended to the lower deck and woke a dozing cook who poured lukewarm coffee into a chipped mug for me. I returned to the upper deck, leaned on the rail, sipped my coffee, and looked across the smooth sea while savoring the caffeine that slowly unclogged my head. Mount Bongao loomed ahead on the horizon about an hour away. I drained the dregs of my coffee and slouched back on a cot, enjoying the caffeine buzz.

"Excuse me. Do you know anything about flights from Bongao to Zamboanga?"

I looked up. It was the American woman. She wore a loose T-shirt and jeans. Her hair was tied in a scarf and she still wore the wrap-around sunglasses. Her makeup was fresh and heavy.

"Yes, I do," I said. "I've taken the flight many times. What do you want to know?"

"How often do planes fly?"

"Once a day on Tuesday and Saturday. There should be a flight this afternoon at four, but it doesn't always arrive." I paused. "I thought you were returning to Zamboanga by ship?"

"I changed my mind. I've seen enough islands and ocean. They become rather predictable after awhile. Is the airlines office in Bongao?"

"Yes. You can't miss it. It's a few doors down from the wharf."

"Thank you." She turned and walked toward her cabin.

A few moments later, Leung joined me and asked, "What did she want?"

Normally I would've politely told him it was none of his business, but I surmised there was a reason for his question.

"She asked about flights to Zamboanga."

"Good. I told her she must leave the ship at Bongao. I think you know why."

"I think I do."

"We'll reach Bongao in about thirty minutes." He left.

The American woman was standing beside me when the heavy gangplank was lowered onto the wharf at Bongao. "The Philippines Air Lines office is about six doors down the street on the right," I told her. "You can't miss it."

She thanked me and I followed her down the gangplank. I walked to the post office and picked up my mail. My long hair and beard were garnering more than the usual stares as I made my way down Bongao's only street, so I decided a change was in order. I visited my favorite barber and after he clipped and shaved me into respectability I went to visit Father Raquet, the local priest.

"Who's the stranger?" he said. His desk was cluttered with papers. "I don't think I've ever seen you short-haired and beardless." Father Raquet was a wiry little man, a few inches over five feet and deeply tanned from his years in the tropics. His hair was gray, his eyes crackling blue and his smile warm and ready. I had met him on my arrival in Tawi-Tawi and we struck an immediate friendship.

"I decided it's time to look respectable before I head for Manila."

"The spare room is vacant and the sun has probably heated up the water tank for a warm shower."

"I won't pass on the shower," I said. "I had a grubby night in a grubby bed on a grubby ship." I took my leave and headed for the spare room.

The warm shower made me drowsy so I caught up on the sleep deprived me the previous night. When I awakened it was late afternoon. I decided to do some shopping for things I couldn't find in Sitangkai's lean shops. I was leaving a Chinese shop—they were all Chinese shops—when I heard the sound of an airplane. I looked up and saw a Philippine Air Lines plane descending to the Sanga-Sanga airstrip. The American woman lucked out.

That evening Father Raquet and I sat in his screened-in lanai contemplating a banana, mango, and papaya dessert prepared by Tia, his cook.

"It looks good," said Father, squeezing juice from a lime over his fruit. "Occasionally Tia does things right. But I guess it's not easy to ruin a dessert of raw fruit." Tia's culinary disasters were an ongoing joke between us. Despite twenty years of cooking for the convento, she hadn't mastered basic culinary skills.

"Any excitement in Bongao since I was last here?" I asked, spooning into my dessert.

"Not much. Father Donahue was down from Jolo for a few days. Oh yes. I almost forgot. There was another visitor. I think it was yesterday or maybe the day before. An American woman was in town."

"Was she from the *Zamboanga Star*?"

"Maybe," said Father. "I saw her in the market place." He took another bite of his dessert. "Her outfit caused quite a stir. She was wearing shorts and a halter. The young men certainly enjoyed it, but I think most people disapproved. You'd think common sense would tell her to dress differently in a traditional Muslim town."

"I agree. When in Rome . . ."

"Exactly. I spoke to her, but she obviously wasn't interested in talking to me. She gave me a chilly 'hello' and turned away. All I saw was a lot of pale skin and blond hair behind big dark sunglasses."

"She was on the ship at Sitangkai when I boarded." I debated whether to tell him about her trysts in the cabin beside me but since the story was probably already circulating through Bongao, I decided to add to the gossip. "She spent most of the night entertaining men in her cabin. Leung made her leave the ship here in Bongao. I think she caught the PAL flight back to Zamboanga."

"Prostitutes occasionally come to town for a few days, but this is the first American one I've heard of."

"I don't think she was a prostitute. She wasn't charging."

"I wonder what her story is."

Christmas was approaching. The Christian holiday meant little in Muslim Tawi-Tawi and not a great deal to me either, but it provided an excuse for a break to Manila after the Zamboanga conference. I hadn't been out of Tawi-Tawi in many months and I was ready for a vacation. I tied up loose ends in Bongao and waited three days for a plane that didn't arrive. I decided to give it one more day. If it didn't appear, I'd take a ship to Zamboanga. Although late, the plane arrived and that evening I was dining at the Bayot Hotel watching the sun explode across the sea behind the distant islands of Basilan. Four days later, I was in Manila.

Manila was its usual sprawling, sweltering, predictable chaos: three million faces, a thousand smells, and a hundred colors; streets crammed with dilapidated taxis, flamboyantly decorated jeepneys, horse-drawn carts and speeding buses; shells of buildings not yet rebuilt from the Japanese war and pontoon bridges still sufficing for those lost to the bombs; shantytowns in the shadows of palatial government buildings; tattered boys hopping on running boards of passing cars selling cigarettes, peanuts, or their sisters' favors; women with huge baskets of produce balanced on their heads and men pushing heavily laden carts through crowded streets; and white-robed priests and nuns materializing here and there like specters from another realm. Frantic, chaotic, smelly, and scary. Manila was exactly what I needed after Sitangkai.

I stayed with a friend and managed to see a bundle of other people who left me hardly a free night. It was strictly a pleasure trip and only once did I talk anthropology. That was an evening when I dined with Father Rodriguez, a Filipino priest from Tawi-Tawi on sabbatical leave to study anthropology at the Ateneo de Manila. I first met him in Bongao when he visited Father Raquet. A bright man with a keen appreciation of anthropology, he had many questions about my research.

We were lingering over coffee when he suggested, "You should visit the school and shelter I'm working with in Tondo."

"Tell me about it."

"Do you know a nun named Sister Josephine?"

"Never heard of her. Should I know her?"

"Probably not," he said, "since you haven't been around Manila much. She's from a wealthy Pennsylvania family and knows a lot of well-heeled people here in the Philippines."

"Part of the oligarchy?"

"Sort of. Most of those people turn me off, but you would never guess her background. She's a very humble woman. She became concerned about the street children several years ago and began ministering to them at a little shelter she established with several lay women. She raised enough money from her family contacts to fund a home for street children in Tondo."

"Do they live there full-time?"

"Yes, it's a shelter and school. The kids are provided food and a place to sleep and classes."

"And what's your connection to it?"

"I've known Sister Josephine several years. I became a volunteer teacher at the shelter when I came to Manila last August. Nuns and priests throughout the city come and help out whenever they can. Lay people are involved too."

"Sounds like a very dedicated group of people."

"They are extremely dedicated. I'm going out there tomorrow. Why don't you come with me? You'll enjoy meeting Sister Josephine. She's a gem. Have you ever been to Tondo?"

"No."

"Come and see how the other half lives."

"You got yourself a date." He promised to pick me up at nine the following morning.

True to his word, Father Rodriguez arrived at nine with his car and driver. We sat in the backseat as the driver navigated through the Manila traffic that strikes terror in the heart of the uninitiated. We inched through the clogged streets and blaring horns and finally made it to Tondo, one of the poorest districts of Manila, consisting mostly of makeshift shacks built of scraps of wood, tin, cardboard, plastic, and anything else that provided a semblance of shelter. Traffic was somewhat less congested, but the streets were almost impassable with deep pot holes and assorted debris. We stopped before a newly constructed wooden wall about six feet high topped with barb wire. A troop of half-naked children emerged from nowhere, most simply curious but some holding out hands for money. Father Rodriguez smiled and spoke to them in Tagalog as he rang a bell above their reach.

Momentarily the door was opened by a young Filipina. She recognized Father Rodriguez and smiled, "Good morning, Father."

"Good morning, Anna Maria. I've brought a friend to visit our school." He introduced me to the young woman who invited us in and closed the door. We stood in a small entry hall filled with paintings of the street-style sold by artists in downtown Manila. Three potted palms added warmth.

"I'll show our guest around," said Father Rodriguez.

"Let me know if you need anything," said the young woman. She smilingly entered a room off the entry hall.

"Nice painting," I said, examining an oil of the Manila Hotel.

"You'll see many more. Sister Josephine loves art and has a big collection." He directed me to a door on the right. "The shelter has three components: a dormitory, a school, and a clinic. The dormitory is limited to resident children. They have priority in the school, but we also admit children from the neighborhood if we have space. The clinic is also for the resident children, but we don't refuse services to any of the needy."

He led me down a hallway to an inner courtyard with playground equipment scattered beneath a banyan tree. We crossed to a room with cots neatly arranged on either side.

"We have four rooms like this," explained Father Rodriguez, "two for boys and two for girls. The children are responsible for maintaining the rooms and, as you can see, they do a good job of it—with a little encouragement from the nuns." Indeed, the room was spotless. The beds were neatly made and beside each was a small chest of drawers.

"For many of the children who come here, this is their first time to sleep in a bed."

Next we visited a dining room decorated with children's art and furnished with tables, chairs, and potted plants. Noises and aromas from an adjoining room revealed a kitchen. We peeked into a classroom where children were learning the geography of the Philippines taught by a young nun, aided by a large map covering the front wall. We then visited the clinic where a Filipino doctor was treating sores on the legs of a small, undernourished, frightened-looking boy. Father Rodriguez introduced me to the doctor, explaining that he volunteered two mornings a week at the clinic.

"And this is José," said the doctor. "He joined us yesterday." The child appraised us suspiciously and unsmilingly.

After we left the clinic, Father Rodriguez asked, "Are you ready for *merienda*?"

"A cup of coffee would be great."

He led me to a small lounge furnished with comfortable rattan furniture and decorated with more paintings and sculptures from Sister Josephine's collection.

"She certainly has an eye for art," I said, admiring an Ifugao carving.

"She's a remarkable woman. This place exists because of her and her inexhaustible energy. Not to mention that she's a great fund-raiser. And a deeply religious woman. She recently returned from a renewal retreat in Mindanao. She works herself to a frazzle and must go into seclusion for spiritual renewal periodically. I don't know how the woman does it all. Too bad she's not here. I'm sure you'd like her."

"I'm sorry I missed her."

"Yes, and you could have met her sister. She's visiting Sister Josephine and touring the Philippines. Another remarkable woman."

He told me more about the shelter, and our conversation drifted to anthropological matters as I accepted a second cup of coffee. The young woman who greeted our arrival brought a plate of cookies. Several workers came into the lounge for coffee and departed after small conversations. As we were agreeing that it was time to leave, we heard voices and laughter in the entry hall.

"You're in luck," said Father Rodriguez. "I think it's Sister Josephine."

A nun dressed in flowing white robes swept into the room. Her radiant face and large blue eyes beamed from her sea of white. With her was a blond woman dressed in an attractive yellow muumuu. "Father Rodriguez," said the nun. "How good to see you. And you have brought a visitor."

"This is a pleasant surprise," said Father. He introduced me.

Sister Josephine smiled and warmly shook my hand. "And this is my sister Evelyn. She's been traveling throughout the Philippines."

"And a brave woman she is," added Father Rodriguez, "traveling all alone."

"Nothing brave about that," said Evelyn. "Filipinos are so hospitable. I've yet to experience any danger."

"We didn't expect to see you," Father Rodriguez said to Sister Josephine. "They told us you were at Malacañang."

"I was but the meeting was cancelled. Some unexplained crisis came up. Probably the First Lady heard about a shoe sale downtown." She laughed. "But it worked out well. I'm able to see you and your friend." She smiled at me. "But I badly need some coffee—and some sustenance. I'm ravenous."

She went to the coffee maker and filled a cup. She returned to the chair beside me and placed her cup on the table. When she stirred her coffee and reached for a cookie, I noticed the little finger of each hand was missing.

She saw me looking at her hands. She raised her hands and wiggled her fingers at me. "You've heard of 'six-fingered people'?"

Her sister raised her hands also and wiggled her fingers. She, too, was missing each little finger. She laughed, "We belong to the four-fingered clan—a genetic kink in our family that's passed through the female line."

"You accomplish so much with eight fingers," said Father Rodriguez, "I can't imagine what you'd do with ten!" They all laughed.

I reached across the table and helped myself to another cookie.

Agents of Change

He was tall and blond and probably the high school football captain. She was shorter, but also blond and with a prettiness that said high school cheerleader or homecoming queen, or both. He majored in political science and her B.A. was in English. They were part of the first wave of Peace Corps volunteers that arrived in the Philippines during my first year in Tawi-Tawi.

I heard about them before I met them. The arrival of strangers, especially white ones, always reached me via the invisible telegraph system that connected the scattered islands of Tawi-Tawi. I was at the remote Lioboran moorage when I learned of them. My Sama Dilaut friend Masa sailed in from Bongao that evening and invited me to eat with his family.

He pulled a piece of fish from the cooking pot, handed it to me and announced, "Two Americans arrived in Bongao, but they're not your race." By "race" he meant they didn't have red hair. Sometime earlier Masa decided that white Americans could be divided into races based on hair color.

"Are you sure they're Americans?" I asked, taking the fish. "How many? Men or women?"

"One man and one woman," he said, pulling another piece of fish from the pot for his wife. He passed pieces to his sons and we sat back to eat. "They were speaking English with Father Raquet. They seemed like Americans."

"Are they tourists?" I asked curiously. Outside visitors to Tawi-Tawi were rare in those days.

"I don't know," he said. "They had lots of boxes. I think they plan to stay awhile. They aren't very beautiful."

I discounted his last comment since the Sama Dilaut thought most whites weren't very beautiful. Their pale, sometimes sunburnt skin and faded hair made them less than attractive to Sama Dilaut eyes.

A couple weeks later I was in Bongao and met the Peace Corps couple in the marketplace where I was trying to find some typing paper. I'd just left Masa's boat and was dressed Sama Dilaut style—barefoot, shorts, and turban. They looked me over appraisingly, and then opened big smiles and approached me with outstretched hands.

"Good morning," I said. "You must be the Americans I heard about." We shook hands and acknowledged we'd heard of one another.

The man said, "I'm Jeff Hudson and this is my wife Rebecca."

"Are you vacationing here?" I asked.

"Not quite," said Rebecca, speaking for the first time. "Our purpose is a little more serious than that." She smiled.

"We're with the Peace Corps," explained her husband.

"I didn't know any Peace Corps people were coming. We usually get wind of such things down here before they happen."

"It was a late decision by the regional office," said Jeff. "This area's been overlooked and is definitely in need of some assistance." I wasn't sure what assistance two young college grads fresh from the States could offer Bongao, but I didn't say so.

"What kind of work will you be doing here?" I asked.

"Community development," replied Rebecca.

"And what's that entail?"

"You're the anthropologist," laughed Jeff. "You should know. We read quite a bit of anthropology during our training program and, no offence, but I must admit some of it seemed a little naive."

I repressed a barb about naiveté and said, "I know about community development, but I was wondering what you have in mind for Bongao."

"Economic development, agriculture, family planning—that sort of thing," replied Rebecca. "The usual community development stuff."

"We'll begin with agriculture," added Jeff. "Economics is the basis of every society and any change must begin there." I recognized a standard line found in most introductory anthropology textbooks. "New varieties of seed corn will do well in this soil. If we can establish it as a crop, we can provide more income for the local people as well as a more nutritious food for their diets."

"Do you really think corn will go over here? A few people raise it, but only to supplement their diets. Improvements in staple crops like cassava, dry rice or bananas might go over better." I was trying to be helpful.

"I'm sure you know the boat people," said Rebecca, "but we've been studying the land people. We've researched the local economic system and are convinced that improvements in corn will add greater nourishment to diets and more money to the economy."

In one month they'd researched the local economic system and dietary needs. I'd been in Tawi-Tawi almost six months and was just beginning to glean some of the intricacies of the Sama Dilaut socio-cultural system. Maybe I was simply slow.

They seemed like nice people, but our introduction was off on the wrong foot, so after a few harmless words I left, saying I was sure we'd meet again. They hoped to see me soon and disappeared into the marketplace. I continued my search for typing paper.

◆ ◆ ◆

During the next few weeks, I occasionally saw the Hudsons in Bongao; we exchanged a few words and went about our separate affairs. One morning I was waiting for the post office to open. A note on the door announced the postmaster would return in twenty minutes. The Hudsons approached me.

"Isn't the post office open?" asked Rebecca, unhappily.

"The postmaster isn't here. He should be back in a few minutes."

"Typical," said Jeff. "We've been here several times during business hours and he was gone. I'm afraid he's typical of the bureaucracy of this country." He shook his head sadly.

"He manages the post office by himself," I said, "and occasionally has to leave. He's actually quite responsible. He's been good about handling my mail."

Rebecca looked at me doubtfully and sat on the makeshift bench beside me. Jeff joined us and said, "I guess we have no choice but to wait. We're expecting an important document from the regional office."

"How's the corn project coming along?" I asked.

"Great," said Jeff, enthusiastically. "I talked two farmers into trying the new variety."

"We expected problems convincing even one to try it, so we're really pleased at having two," added Rebecca.

"We're working with them closely. If their crop is successful, next season more will try it and eventually the whole area will see its benefits. Latin America has had some spectacular results with this particular variety, but it hasn't been tried much in Southeast Asia."

"Sounds promising," I said, not really sure the Hudsons were going to make corn-eaters out of the Tawi-Tawi people. But I didn't say so.

Apparently my doubts showed. Jeff said, "I don't think you're sold on the project."

I shrugged. "I'm not sure it's possible to change people's diets unless there's a great advantage for them to do so. People are really conservative about food. But if you can improve the local diets, I'll be the first to congratulate you. I hope it works. Any other projects in the wind?"

"The corn's taking most of our time," said Rebecca, "but we'll begin working on the dogs soon."

"The dogs?"

"Haven't you noticed them?" asked Jeff.

"I've noticed them, but I'm not sure what you have in mind."

"They're a serious problem," said Rebecca. "They're diseased and filthy, nothing but skin and bones covered with disgusting sores. I've even seen them eating human excrement." She shuddered slightly. "They howl all night and it's impossible to get a good night's sleep."

I shared her views about the Bongao dogs. They were, indeed, a sorry lot of mangy, half-starved curs that howled at the slightest provocation. I really hadn't considered them a major problem though.

"What do you plan to do about them?"

"We haven't decided yet," said Jeff. "But something must be done. They're a major nuisance, not to mention a health hazard."

"Have you talked to Father Raquet? He might have some thoughts on the subject."

They exchanged glances. Jeff said, "No. We don't see much of him. We'd rather not be identified with him. After all, he's a Catholic missionary and this is a Muslim province."

"We're certainly not here to missionize," said Rebecca. I bit my tongue and didn't mention that maybe their plans to change the local culture weren't too different from the way missionaries imposed new religions on people.

I was biased. I liked Father Raquet and had to defend him. "I don't think you know him very well. He's highly respected. During his twenty-plus years here, he's never converted a Muslim—and he's not likely to do so. He's so busy helping people that he hasn't time to be concerned about their religion. Believe me, if you want to make inroads into the local communities, it would be well for you to know him."

"We're not Catholics, you know," said Rebecca.

"Neither am I. In fact, I think Father Raquet considers me a hopeless atheist."

"Aren't you concerned that your research might be colored by your association with a Catholic priest?" asked Jeff.

"I don't think you understand his role in this community. Some of his best friends are local *imams* and *hajjis*."

"We appreciate your advice," said Rebecca.

I wasn't sure they did, but was prevented from saying so by the arrival of the postmaster. He apologized for being away, his wife was ill and he'd been checking on her.

Several days later, I found myself with a day to kill. The boat I'd planned to take to an outer moorage wasn't leaving until evening and I was uncommitted until then. I decided to call on the Hudsons. They'd extended invitations several times but I'd never visited them. I found their house and knocked on its closed front door.

"Who is it?" It was Rebecca's voice.

I identified myself. She unlocked the door and peeked through the crack.

"I came by to chat a bit if you're not busy."

"Jeff's not here."

"I didn't come specifically to see him, but if it's a bad time I'll come back some other time."

"No. That's alright," she said, opening the door so I could enter. "I was about to make some coffee." She placed a kettle on the kerosene stove. "I've been thinking about home. I'm a little homesick today. Do you ever get homesick?"

"Occasionally," I said, sitting in the chair she suggested. "But it usually doesn't last long. If it does, I dive into work and forget it."

"It's one of those days when it would be nice to talk to someone back home. Some people here speak English but we don't have a lot in common. I really miss good intellectual discussions, don't you?"

"Sometimes," I said. "But I have friends here who share some of my interests. And Father Raquet is always up for a lively debate."

"Maybe if we spoke Sinama, it would be different," she mused. She spooned instant coffee into two cups, filled them with hot water, and handed one to me.

"How are the projects going?" I asked.

"Okay," she said, sipping her coffee. "The corn's looking good, but there's not a lot we can do until it's harvested and people see the results. The mayor's having trouble finding money for the dog pen. He's also having trouble finding volunteers to build it. I suppose we'll end up doing most of the work."

"Any new project in the wind?"

"We're about to begin a birth control pilot project," she said with enthusiasm entering her voice for the first time since I arrived. "You wouldn't believe the size of some of these families. No wonder they're so poor. Every centavo goes to feeding all those kids. Women have time for nothing else but babies. I'll be working with the women and Jeff will work with the men."

I wasn't sure the Tawi-Tawi people were ready for birth control, but I didn't say anything. I changed the subject and asked her what she was doing before she joined the Peace Corps. It was like turning on a water tap that wouldn't stop as she spilled out her life. Obviously homesick, she reminisced about her family and college years. She was from a small city in California where she attended a state university and met Jeff. They married during their senior year and decided a stint in the Peace Corps would be a good honeymoon as well as a chance to help the underprivileged of the world. The more she talked, the more I liked her. She was a genuinely good woman, sincerely concerned about the plight of the downtrodden of the world. She wanted to make a dent in that plight, her motivation for joining the Peace Corps. Jeff shared her concern and they decided that two years of their lives helping others was a small sacrifice in the big scheme of things.

I noticed an open book on the table, *The Portrait of a Lady* by Henry James.

"Do you like Henry James?" I asked.

She laughed. "I actually do now. I had to read him once in an American lit class and thought he was the most boring writer possible. But for some reason, over here, I find him enjoyable. I can hardly put the book down."

"I know what you mean. I think it might be a form of homesickness. I'm reading novels here that bored me stiff back home. I even read *Humphry Clinker*. Have you ever tried that one?"

She laughed. "I'm not that desperate yet. But give me another month and I might try it."

For the next hour we discussed literature. When I left the house, I had very different feelings about the Hudsons. Their intentions were obviously admirable, although some of their methods seemed naïve. But I'd made my share of cultural gaffes when I arrived in Tawi-Tawi, so I knew where they were coming from. I decided to stop giving them advice and let them find their own way. Besides, at times I sounded too self-righteous for my own good.

About two weeks later, I ran into Jeff in the marketplace. He saw me before I saw him and greeted me with one of his big smiles.

"Good to see you," he shouted across the busy corridor. "How's your research going? Haven't seen you in ages."

"I've been busy," I said, as we approached one another. "How are you and Rebecca?"

"Fine, fine. Really busy the past few weeks. Really pleased with things."

"What's happening since I last saw you?"

"We're moving right along with the dog problem. The mayor's very cooperative."

"Tell me about it."

"We met with the mayor and some members of the town council after we saw you. They agreed the dogs are a nuisance and a serious health problem. We proposed that all the strays be rounded up and placed in a pen which the mayor has agreed to build. They'll be penned-up for a week and those that aren't claimed will be euthanized."

"Have you talked to many people about it?"

"Enough to know they agree it's a problem."

"The Sama Dilaut have a belief that dogs can sense the presence of spirits, and they—"

"That's a quaint belief," he laughed. "I've never heard any Muslims say anything about spirits and dogs."

"Have you started rounding them up yet?"

"Not yet. I talked to the mayor this morning and he expects to have money for the pen by the end of the week."

"And how's the corn project?"

"Great. You wouldn't believe the size of that corn. It's twice the height of the local varieties and looks like it's going to have about three times the yield. Everyone envies the farmers growing it. By next season, we expect to have the entire village planting it. It's amazing what a difference a little modern know-how can make in these villages. After the harvest is in, we'll teach the women some new recipes for preparing corn."

"Sounds like you're going great guns."

"Couldn't be more pleased," he smiled proudly. "And this is just the beginning. We have plans for better house construction, birth control, fishing—this should be quite a different place when we leave."

"Indeed."

"I must run," he said. "I promised to meet Rebecca at ten. Come by and see us. Sorry I missed you last week when you stopped by." He disappeared into the crowd.

The next month was a busy one. I was doing a census of the Sama Dilaut and was away from Bongao most of the month. One morning I awakened to a pouring rain drenching everything in my little houseboat. I felt weary of what I was doing, hungry for some creature comforts, and lonely for people from my own culture. I decided I needed a break from Tawi-Tawi. I told Masa I was going away for awhile, took down my nipa roof, put up my sail and headed for Bongao through the gray skies and choppy seas. I planned to catch the first available plane, ship or launch headed toward Manila. It was late afternoon when I arrived in Bongao, soaked and chilled to the bone. I found my way to Father Raquet's convento where I was greeted warmly. Our conversation extended into dinner and beyond. The long day took its toll and I found my way to bed for a sleep that was uninterrupted until morning.

When I awakened Father Raquet was already out, so I fixed myself a leisurely breakfast. After too many cups of coffee, I decided to walk to the wharf and see what kind of transportation might be available. Half-way down Bongao's muddy street, I met Jeff.

"God, but it's good to see an American face," he said. "Where've you been?"

He'd never greeted me so warmly. "I've been busy in the outer islands. How have you been?"

"Up and down. Mostly down at the minute. Let me buy you a cup of coffee."

I was already sloshing with caffeine but accepted his invitation. We walked to a little nearby restaurant, found seats, and ordered.

"So what's happening?" I asked.

He sipped his coffee. "You wouldn't believe the fiasco that's grown out of the corn project. A couple weeks ago, we harvested the corn. It was a tremendous harvest. The men who grew it had four times the harvest of other farmers. And big ears, too. Twice the size of the others. Everyone in the village was excited and wanted seed for the next planting. Rebecca organized a group of women and showed them different ways to cook it."

He paused and ordered another cup of coffee.

"It was delicious corn. The roasting ears were exactly like those I remember from my grandfather's farm. Rebecca prepared dishes for the women. They all agreed they were delicious and were eager to try them at home. Then we noticed their enthusiasm began fading. The farmers who wanted seed corn didn't say anything more about it. The corn we distributed to the village wasn't eaten. When we asked about it, we got all kinds of answers. Some said they were saving it for a special occasion. Some said they ate it. Some said they hadn't got around to it yet. None of them were telling the truth. You wouldn't believe what finally came out."

He paused. I shrugged and gave him a blank look.

"They didn't like the taste of it!" he said. "Can you believe it? It didn't taste like their old corn. And it didn't have the color of their old corn when they cooked it. I couldn't believe it. It tasted far better than that ratty corn they grow here and it's much more nutritious."

"People are very conservative about food," I ventured.

"And now none of them want to plant it," he continued. "It gives four times the yield and is far superior to the old corn, but no one wants to plant it. I overestimated these people."

"Maybe you underestimated tradition. If someone tried to talk you into eating something that didn't taste like it was supposed to, you'd probably resist too."

"But even if I didn't like it, I could see the greater yields. I could always sell the surplus."

"But who's going to buy it, if no one likes it? Besides, corn's not a cash crop here and not a favorite food. Most people grow a little for occasional variation in their diets."

"But why can't they see the potential? It grows well in this soil. They could get a lot more food for less effort."

"Rice grows tremendously well in parts of the States, but you don't see Americans becoming rice eaters, do you?"

"I've had it with these people. I'm tired of wasting my time."

"Why don't you try working with some improved types of rice or cassava? You might have better luck."

"Why waste my time? I'm sure it wouldn't taste right." He stood. "I gotta go." He paid for the coffee, muttered a farewell, gave me a forced smile, and left.

I wandered down to the wharf and found a ship leaving for Zamboanga that evening.

I was in Manila a couple of weeks. When I returned to Bongao, my first stop was the post office. I picked up my mail and sat on the bench outside to read it. Halfway through my first letter I was interrupted.

"Long time, no see." I looked up and saw Jeff approaching.

"Good morning," I said. "How's everything?"

"About as good as can be expected," he said, removing his hat and sitting beside me. "I don't know how you keep your sanity in this place."

"Still busy with community development projects?"

"An exercise in futility is more like it. If I didn't believe so strongly in what we're trying to do, I'd throw in the towel."

"More disappointments?"

"I keep running into this mentality that hasn't evolved beyond the Stone Age. Remember our plans to deal with the dog problem?"

I said I remembered.

"The mayor kept putting us off. Said he couldn't find money for the dog pen. Then he said he couldn't find anyone to build it. We finally built most of it ourselves. No one volunteered to round up the dogs, so we did that too. We had most of the strays in the pen but when we returned the next morning they were gone. We thought they'd broken through the pen, so we repaired it and rounded them up again. You can't believe how great the nights were without howling dogs. The streets were cleaner too. Then one morning we went to the pen and they were gone again. This time it was obvious someone had cut the wire."

He paused for a comment from me, but I had nothing to say.

"I questioned several people about it, but of course they claimed to know nothing. They all said it was awful that the dogs escaped. We fixed the pen again, rounded up the dogs once more, and patrolled the area during the night. But eventually the fence was cut again and the dogs got out."

"Did you ever find out who did it?"

"Not for certain, but I have my suspicions. Rebecca and I, of course, were doing all the work—repairing the fence and rounding up the dogs. Everyone else was busy when we asked for help. Finally, we realized we were fighting a losing battle and gave up. Stories began coming back to us. You wouldn't believe why they were letting the dogs out."

"Maybe I would."

He continued. "These people believe that when dogs howl at night it keeps away bad spirits. And because of that stupid superstition they don't want to get rid of the dogs. Can you believe it? What do you do when you're confronted with a mentality like that?"

"Respect it?" I suggested.

"I'm beginning to understand why this place is centuries behind the rest of the world."

"Maybe different from the rest of the world, but not necessarily behind."

"I'm afraid I don't share your romantic notions of the primitive life," he said, standing up.

"Not romantic, relative."

He looked at me exasperatedly and entered the post office. I returned to my letters.

The next morning, Jeff came to the convento where I was
lingering over breakfast while plotting a way to spend the day.
He saw me through the open door before I saw him.

"I was hoping you'd be here," he said, entering.

"What brings you around so early?"

"Business," he said, settling into a chair. "And to ask a
favor. I need to go to Banabana this morning for another birth
control seminar but our outboard motor's on the blink again. I
was wondering if we could borrow your boat."

I wasn't enthusiastic about loaning my boat so I said, "I'm
free this morning and can take you over."

"I hate to put you out, but we really need to get over there.
We should leave soon."

I gulped a final gulp of coffee, found my hat, and we
walked toward my boat. We stopped to pick up Rebecca and
were soon sailing toward Banabana, an island across the channel
from Bongao.

En route, the Hudsons explained their birth control project.
It was a pilot project and if it worked in Banabana, they
planned to expand it to other villages. They'd had two meetings
with the villagers. Rebecca met with the women and Jeff with
the men. The first meeting dealt with the problems of large
families and overpopulation. They explained the diminishing

resources of the islands and the expenses of a large family. Using charts they showed how rapidly the population was growing and the serious consequences if something wasn't done. They graphically illustrated the expenses of a large family and explained what a family of four could have as opposed to a family of eight. Village turnout was excellent and everyone seemed genuinely concerned about the problem. The second seminar was about birth control methods. Again Jeff met with the men and Rebecca the women. With graphic aids, they illustrated how fertilization occurs and how it can be prevented with contraceptives. In those days the pill was just emerging and condoms were still the most widespread method of birth control. They educated their respective seminars about condoms and distributed some to the attendees. That was two weeks ago and today the Hudsons were returning for a third seminar to see how things were going and distribute a new supply of condoms.

When we moored at the small wharf, we were met by a group of children playing with long, white balloons.

"My God!" said Rebecca. "Those are condoms!"

"Damn!" exclaimed Jeff. They hurried down a path toward the village, leaving me to secure the boat.

I wasn't interested in joining them, so I stayed with the boat and cleaned the hull while I waited. Several kids came over to see what I was doing and told me about the great balloons the Hudsons gave their parents. They'd been playing with them for days, breaking many but they still had plenty more.

About twenty minutes later, the Hudsons were back, stony-faced and silent.

"Let's go back to Bongao," said Jeff, helping Rebecca into the boat. They sat at the bow with their backs to me. We headed toward Bongao.

After about five minutes of silence, Jeff said, "It appears that not a single person tried the condoms."

"Did you find out why?"

He sighed. "They want to have babies. They told us they want to have as many children as they can. They said it's Allah's will that people have babies. What can you do when you're confronted with a mentality like that?"

After a few moments of silence, I said, "I'm going to be candid with you. I hope I don't offend you, but I'll risk it because I like you two. If you'd taken more time to learn about the local culture, you'd realize that big families are desired here. It's the only support people have. If they don't have big families to care for them when they're sick, when they need help or when they're old, who's going to do it? There aren't any government programs to help. You wouldn't be interested in birth control either if you were in their position."

"Why didn't they tell us that?" asked Rebecca, sadly. "We would've understood."

"Probably because you never asked. You came as visitors to the village, persons of authority. And you surely know enough about local etiquette by now to realize that such visitors are treated with utmost respect. You don't disagree with them, you don't challenge them. You tolerate them and hope they'll go away so you can continue what you were doing before they arrived."

They sat quietly, glum and sad-faced as I steered the boat toward Bongao. When we neared the wharf, Rebecca leaned forward and her back began shaking. "Oh my god," I thought. "Now she's crying."

Then suddenly, she burst into laughter. "Condom balloons! They gave the friggin' condoms to the kids!"

Jeff looked at her, startled at first and then he began laughing. "They'd been breaking them for days! Condoms scattered all over the place!" He guffawed, "We should write the Trojan company and tell them we found a new market for their product!"

"We introduced a new toy!" howled Rebecca. "It's our only successful project so far!"

They roared with laughter, obviously having found an outlet for their frustration. It was infectious and I was happy to laugh with them. By the time we reached Bongao, tears streamed down our faces as we laughed hysterically. After we moored the boat, Jeff said, "This calls for a celebration. Drinks on me."

We walked up the path to a little waterfront restaurant, still laughing. A few passersby stared at us nervously as if their initial impression that Americans were a bit crazy was being verified. Others saw us laughing and laughed with us.

At the bar, we ordered coffee after deciding it was too early for beer. The Hudsons joked about their failed dog eradication program and their unsuccessful attempt to make corn a staple in Tawi-Tawi. During the second cup of coffee, they began to sober up.

"We had such vague instructions from the regional office when they sent us down here," said Jeff. "We were originally scheduled to go to an Ilocano village in Luzon, but at the last minute, they changed their minds and sent us here. The training we received in the States was mostly about Christian Filipinos. We didn't know anything about the Muslims. In fact, I never knew there were Muslims in the Philippines until the last week of our training program."

Rebecca added, "They gave us a list of possible projects to explore with the Bongao mayor. He wasn't at all helpful and obviously didn't know what to do with us."

Jeff looked at me with a sad smile and said, "We haven't exactly set the world on fire, have we?"

"But you've learned a lot," I said. "Now maybe you're ready to tackle something the community wants—rather than something you think it should have."

That opportunity came a few days later. The village of Banabana where the Hudsons distributed condoms hosted the only school on the little island. It was suddenly without teachers when one of them died of a heart attack and the other, his wife, resigned in grief. The headman of the village and three elders visited the Hudsons a few days later. I was at their house when they arrived. The headman politely thanked them for their efforts to help his village, tactfully not mentioning the failed birth control project. Rebecca served refreshments and after exhausting small talk, the headman approached the reason for the visit.

"We no longer have teachers on our island and our children cannot attend school," he said, sadly. "We would greatly appreciate it if you would teach our children. We want them to learn English. If they are to succeed beyond the village, they must know English. My generation grew up under American rule and learned English, but the younger generation is not learning it."

"But we speak only a little Sinama," said Jeff. "We would have trouble teaching the other subjects."

"We've thought of that," said the headman. "Several older people in the village speak English but they cannot read or write. They could help in the classroom as interpreters while you learn Sinama and the children learn English."

The Hudsons looked at one another. "We'll have to discuss it," said Jeff.

"I understand," said the headman. "We'll provide a house for you if you decide to come. We'll wait for your decision." After some polite departing words, they left.

It wasn't a difficult decision for the Hudsons. They mutually agreed that teaching English would be a productive way to spend their remaining contract with the Peace Corps. A few days later, I helped them move to a little house in Banabana where they were warmly welcomed by the villagers. They began teaching the next day and the schoolhouse was filled with eager students.

The Hudsons found their forte. They loved teaching and as the children learned English, they learned Sinama. I visited them several weeks later and was amazed at their fluency. The village adored them. Their home became the social center of Banabana and their popularity assured invitations to all the important ceremonies and religious holidays in the village.

Despite their popularity, however, the Hudsons left Tawi-Tawi before their Peace Corps contract expired. Rebecca became pregnant and they wanted to return to the States for the birth of their baby. The villagers hosted a big farewell party. Father Raquet and I were invited. The following day, we saw them off on the *Jolo J* at the Bongao wharf with most of the people from Banabana. Many tears flowed, including my own. We had become close friends and I was genuinely sorry to see them leave.

After the Hudsons left, local farmers still grew their corn in the same old way, Bongao's mangy dogs still howled all night long, and Banabana babies still arrived with great regularity. But some things were different. Many youth of Banabana now spoke English and, perhaps more importantly, the little village held fond memories of the young American couple who once lived among them and introduced their children to a world beyond Tawi-Tawi.

The Man in the House on the River

Masa picked up a skull and turned it slowly in his hands. "This is my grandmother," he mused. "She was a good woman." I remembered the gravedigger scene from *Hamlet*.

We were at Bunabuna'an, the small island that served as cemetery for the Sama Dilaut. Two days previously, Masa's sister-in-law died from childbirth complications after the family exhausted their traditional pharmacopoeia on her. Shamans were called in too. One chanted *kata-kata* for three nights, but even the sacred chants of the ancients couldn't save her. The large flotilla of houseboats regaled in flags and banners and filled with drums and gongs that accompanied the funeral boat was testimony to her loss. We arrived at Bunabuna'an the previous evening and moored overnight on the reef surrounding the island. Now in the early morning, I was helping Masa and his relatives prepare the grave for burial.

We removed the gravemarkers and scraped away sand from the boards covering the shallow crypt which housed the bones and grave goods of deceased family members. The bones were neatly piled, but one skeleton remained within its rotted shroud, its flesh having long ago decomposed. The old shaman overseeing the burial directed Masa to remove the shroud from the skeleton and stack its bones beside the others. That's when he recognized his grandmother's skull. He and his brother cleaned the grave, retained some grave goods, but discarded others that had served their function, such as a bottle of mother's milk near an infant's bones.

"It's ready," Masa announced. He stepped from the grave and we returned to the beach where the houseboats were moored. The mourners in the funeral boat were still singing the flattering songs to the deceased's spirit they had sung for two days. To do otherwise might displease the spirit and bring it back to haunt the living. When Masa told them it was time to take the corpse to the grave, a fresh chorus of wails filled the boat, echoed by other mourners in nearby boats.

Masa and two of his cousins lifted the white shrouded corpse from the boat and gently carried it through the shallow reef waters to the beach where mourners tearfully followed them to the cemetery. I stood aside, absorbing the scene, unwilling to intrude with my camera and notepad into the pain of the bereaved.

At the cemetery, the body was lowered into the grave while the family knelt and wept. The shaman loosened the shroud around the mouth of the corpse and held smoking incense near it. He addressed the spirit, telling it we had performed the proper rituals and asking its blessings. He then invited the spirit to join the ancestors who preceded it to the spirit realm. Mourners approached the open grave and uttered a few final flattering words to the corpse. Then Masa and the old shaman replaced the boards atop the crypt and covered them with sand. A beautiful, newly carved grave marker was placed atop the grave and with a libation of fresh water, the shaman uttered a final prayer. Slowly, the mourners returned to their houseboats and I was left with Masa and two of his cousins. We wandered among the palm-shaded graves, the men commenting on who was buried where. Masa stopped and looked more carefully at two graves.

"Some of the gravemarkers are missing," he said.

"Yes," agreed a cousin. "Old Makata had a beautiful marker. It was carved by our grandfather. It should be here but it's gone."

They examined nearby graves.

"And the marker of Lanaka is gone," said Masa. "And Damati." He added ominously, "The ancestors will be angry."

"This is not good," said a cousin, apprehensively. "It's time to go. They're waiting for us in the boats."

The men quietly walked through the shaded graves and with almost audible relief entered the sun-filled beach where the boats waited in the shallow reef waters. I followed them.

About a week later I was sitting in an outriggered dugout moving against the slow current of the Malum River, one of the few streams on Tawi-Tawi Island big enough to be called a river. Nena Sanchez, a Filipina friend and fellow anthropologist, was visiting me from Manila and looking up a distant relative, Ramon Mañales, a captain in the Philippine Constabulary who lived on the river. She invited me to accompany her, partly because she didn't know the man and didn't want to be alone with him if he turned out to be a creep. A launch transported us to the mouth of the river. From there we transferred to an outrigger canoe, and now two burly Sama men paddled us upstream, exerting a lot of muscle against the current and sharing the broad smiles worn so easily by their people. It was mid-afternoon. We would return to Bongao the next day.

This was new territory for me. Most of my time with the Sama Dilaut was spent on the sea and I rarely ventured on land unless they did. I'd never explored the rivers of Tawi-Tawi that began as trickling streams in the interior mountains and became small rivers emptying into the surrounding sea. Nena and I sat between the paddlers at either end of the boat and watched the dense jungle vegetation slide by.

I curiously and somewhat nervously scanned the river for crocodiles that reportedly still populated remote parts of the island. I'd yet to see one, but every drifting log captured my attention. The jungle met the river on both sides with an occasional small beach or sandbar breaking the monotony of the water and vegetation. A discordant chorus of insect and bird calls surrounded us. Occasionally a curious monkey appeared in the trees to watch us pass and then disappeared into the jungle. Overhead a typical cerulean Tawi-Tawi sky hosted a brilliant sun and a collection of clouds. We said little, enjoying and absorbing our outing.

We rounded a bend in the river and saw our destination. Built of thatch and bamboo on piles at the edge of the river, the house stood alone blending comfortably into the forest behind it. A spacious lanai spread over the water with steps leading to a small dock below. A man dressed in military fatigues held a menacing automatic rifle and quietly watched our approach. One of our paddlers shouted that we were guests of Captain Mañales. As we neared the small dock, a man came from the house and greeted us. We secured our boat and climbed the steps to the lanai.

The man approaching us might have been good-looking if he shed about thirty pounds and worked on his grooming. His hair was oiled to his head and his left little fingernail was considerably longer than the others. A single black hair erupted from a mole on his lower right cheek.

"I'm so glad you arrived safely," he said with an outstretched hand. "You must be Nena."

"Yes," said Nena, accepting his hand. "And you are Ramon. And this is my friend and fellow anthropologist." She introduced us and we shook hands. His hand was boneless.

"I hope your trip was comfortable," he said. "Come inside. I have refreshments for you."

We followed him inside. I'm not sure what I expected, but it wasn't what I encountered. The large room we entered opened to the lanai. Three doors led off the back to what I later discovered were bedrooms. An open ceiling revealed the underside of the thatched roof. The floor was split bamboo and the exterior walls were constructed local-style from woven coconut fronds. Nothing surprising so far. However, in each of the four corners of the room, a stuffed monkey chained to a pedestal stared at us blankly. Hanging from either sidewall were two large crocodile skins, complete with heads and tails. Each was flanked by two exceptionally long stuffed snakes. Three boar heads baring ferocious tusks glared down from above the doors to the lanai. The halves of a huge bivalve filled one corner and above them hung a menacing six-foot sawfish. In the center of the room, a large bamboo cage was filled with strangely quiet colorful birds; they, too, were dead. Four beautiful, lethal-looking krisses adorned the wall between the open lanai doors. A dining table, central to the room, was set for three with an assortment of biscuits and fruits.

Mañales went to a side door and shouted something in Tagalog I couldn't understand. We sat at the table and soon a smiling young man appeared with three glasses of guava juice. As we ate, we said the usual inanities people say when they first meet. After consuming our refreshments, Mañales directed us to the more comfortable chairs at the front of the room.

"You must like monkeys," I said, surveying the stuffed primates.

"I find them amusing," Mañales replied.

"Are those crocodiles from the river?" I asked.

"Yes, they are. Taxidermy is my hobby."

"And the krisses. What a beautiful collection. Where'd they come from?"

"Here and there from local Moros," he replied, dismissively.

I noticed for the first time three large wooden carvings in a back corner. I walked over and examined them more closely. They were Sama Dilaut gravemarkers. "Where did these come from?" I asked.

"A man was selling them in Batu-Batu. Some sort of pagan carvings. I bought them from him."

"They're Sama Dilaut gravemarkers. I was recently at their cemetery and some of them were missing. Do you know the man who sold them to you?"

"No. I never saw him before. And I'll probably never see him again." He turned to Nena, "Tell me about our dear cousin Leonora. Is it true that she will soon marry?"

He obviously wasn't interested in discussing the gravemarkers. He and Nena talked about family matters while I observed the macabre room more closely. It was a strange man who put it together. I instinctively disliked him. I had an admitted prejudice against the Philippine Constabulary because of their sometimes brutal treatment of the local people. I'd met some good men among them, but this wasn't one of them.

After exhausting family gossip, Mañales invited us to see his grounds. He led us through a rear hallway to a small lanai at the back where the jungle was cleared. The clearing was partially occupied by a small barracks that housed PC men. Two of them lounged on a porch and nodded acknowledgments at us. A small building to the left of the barracks was secured with a large padlock on its door.

Mañales saw me looking at it and said, "That's where I do my taxidermy."

We returned to the house where Nena and I were shown our bedrooms and a bathroom— literally a "bath" room, the toilet was an outhouse in the back. We followed Mañales's suggestion that we might want to rest before dinner.

I entered my room and closed the door, appreciative of the first privacy I'd had all day. The room was sparsely furnished with a single bed enveloped in a mosquito net, a small table and a rattan chair. It was thankfully free of dead animals. I parted the mosquito net and lay on the bed, recalling that one of the blessings of life at sea with the Sama Dilaut was the absence of insects. I closed my eyes, remembered that today was my twenty-sixth birthday, and slept.

I awakened at dusk. I found my way to the washroom, splashed water on my face and went to the living room where Mañales and Nena were seated with beers. The room of dead animals was even more macabre in the gathering darkness.

"You're awake," said Mañales. "Would you like a beer?"

"I'd love it. Sorry I slept so late."

"No problem. We're still gossiping about family."

The smiling young man magically appeared with a San Miguel beer for me. Mañales spoke Tagalog to him and he returned minutes later with two kerosene lamps that dispelled some of the room's shadows. Rather startlingly, the lamps revealed three armed guards I'd not noticed before. One stood near the left front door to the lanai and another stood at the back hall. Outside, another paced the lanai overlooking the river.

Mañales saw me looking at them and said, "Don't be alarmed. They're merely precaution. I always have armed men on the property."

"Have you been attacked?"

"Only once, but you never know when these Moros will try something. They hate us."

And not without cause, I thought to myself.

"In Manila," he continued, "they say, 'the only good Moro is a dead Moro.'"

"You surely don't believe that," I said.

"If you were in my line of work, you might believe it."

Nena sensed the growing tension and diplomatically changed the subject. "How long have you been in Tawi-Tawi, Ramon?"

"Five years. Seems like five centuries. That's what my wife says."

"Your wife is here?" I asked.

"Of course not. She'd never come to this backward place."

"Why do you stay here if you don't like it? Can't you transfer?"

"Probably. But the job has perks. We get extra pay for being in a dangerous area."

"Tawi-Tawi dangerous? I've been wandering around here for over a year and never felt any danger."

"Wear my uniform and get a deeper tan and you might change your mind. Here comes dinner." My dislike of the man was growing.

I awakened early the next morning and repacked my small bag. When I entered the living room, Nena was sitting at the table with a cup of coffee.

"You're early," I said.

"Yes. I didn't sleep too well. There's coffee in the kitchen."

As I turned toward the kitchen, the young man who seemed to intuitively know my wishes appeared with a steaming cup of coffee.

I thanked him and sat beside Nena. "Our boat should be here at eight," she reminded me.

"I'm ready," I said, meaningfully.

"I know. This place is slightly creepy."

"More than slightly."

"I really appreciate you coming here with me," she said. "I'm glad I didn't come alone."

"It's been an adventure."

"I'll see if the boat is here." She walked toward the lanai, opened the door, and screamed.

"What is it?" I hurried to her side.

She stared at the threshold. A small monkey dressed in an oversized military fatigue jacket lay in a pool of blood with its throat slit.

Behind us, I heard Mañales. "What is it?" He hurried toward us followed by the houseboy. He stared at the dead monkey and muttered angrily, "Those filthy savages."

"Who did it?" asked Nena.

"The Moro pigs."

"But why?"

"Because they are filthy swine." He shouted in Tagalog and two men came running from the back. I didn't understand what he said, but he was obviously furious at them. He went to the back of the house and shouted orders. I glanced beyond the lanai and saw our boat waiting.

"Are you ready to leave?" asked Nena.

"More than ready."

Mañales returned to the living room. "I don't know how those swine got past the guard. Probably the lazy idiot was sleeping. I must take care of this matter. I think your boat is here."

"I'm sorry about all of this," said Nena. "You've been so kind to put us up. I'll give Leonora your good wishes when I see her."

"Yes, yes," said Mañales, obviously eager for our departure.

We went to our rooms. When we returned to the living room with our bags, Mañales was gone. We descended to the small dock where our boat waited with an additional passenger shaded from the sun by a cloth draped over his head. The paddlers shoved the boat from the dock and we were soon caught in the downstream current.

"I hope you don't mind if this boy accompanies us," said one of the paddlers.

"No," I said. "Who is he?"

The youth turned and removed the covering from his head. It was Mañales's houseboy. He looked terrified and said to me, "I must leave, sir. That is an evil house. I cannot stay there."

"What do you mean 'evil'?" asked Nena. "What has happened?"

"Two nights ago someone left a snake on the front lanai cut in three pieces. And now the monkey."

"But who's doing it?" I asked. "What does it mean?"

"I don't know, but it's very bad. I cannot stay. He is an evil man."

Thanks to the swift current, we soon reached the mouth of the river where the youth left us. Nena and I found a launch headed for Bongao and the following day, she caught a plane for Manila. After seeing her off at the airstrip, I decided to visit Father Raquet, curious to learn what he knew about Ramon Mañales and his strange house on the river.

I knocked on the convento door and Father Raquet's voice invited me inside. I opened the door and saw him sitting in his favorite rattan basket chair.

"Where've you been? I haven't seen you in a spell."

"Here and there. A friend was in town for a few days. We visited one of her relatives who lives on the Malum River. Do you know the river?"

"Yes, but I haven't been up there in years. Not much there as I recall."

"Do you know a Philippine Constabulary captain named Ramon Mañales?"

"Oh yes. He lives up there, doesn't he? Did you meet him?"

"Yes. I stayed overnight at his place." I told him about our visit to the house with all the dead animals.

"I don't think he's a good man," said Father. After a pause, he added, "He's very unpopular with the local people. As you know, the Muslims have always had a rocky relationship with the Christians, and unfortunately most Philippine Constabulary are Christians. Most of them are decent men, but occasionally a bad one comes along and reverses all the good the others have done."

"What's the problem with Mañales?"

"Corrupt, among other things. And a bully. The PC captain of this region normally lives in Batu-Batu where his contingent is stationed, but Mañales chose to build his private house up the river. I've never seen him at Mass."

"He has a thing for taxidermy. His place is filled with dead animals. I think something's going on up there." I told him about the dead monkey dressed in military fatigues and the mutilated snake.

"That doesn't sound good," mused Father. "I wonder who's behind it. Many people dislike him. Not only local people. He's shoved his way into the jurisdiction of other government officials. I heard that when he catches fishermen using dynamite, he confiscates the dynamite, fines the fishermen, and then sells it back to other fishermen." He paused. "But I'm gossiping. I've only heard these things." He paused again. "But experience has taught me that gossip is often rooted in fact. Especially when it comes to corruption."

After I left Father Raquet, I walked down to the waterfront. A tramp freighter was docked at the wharf. Tramps were in their twilight days in those years. Most were rusty old cargo tubs that wandered among the islands buying whatever they could at good prices and selling it elsewhere at a profit. Sometimes women were aboard negotiating their personal wares to the horny local men.

I walked toward the old tub, wondering where it was from. A man cautiously stepped his way down its rickety gangplank. It was Ramon Mañales. He didn't see me. The captain was on deck, a grubby middle-aged European. As I approached he invited me aboard. I had nothing better to do so I joined him on deck. He turned out to be Greek and spoke good English, albeit fractured with a thick accent. When he offered me a drink, I opted for a San Miguel beer while he drank something anonymously brown from a quart bottle.

After a bit of talk about where he'd been and where he was going, I asked him if he knew Captain Mañales.

"Who?"

"Captain Mañales. The man who left your boat a few minutes ago."

"Oh him. So that's his name. Yes, I know him. I buy cigarettes from him."

"Where does he get cigarettes?"

The old Greek smiled at me and said, "You're not that dumb."

"Maybe."

"He's with the PC. My guess is he takes the pick of the crop when he captures smugglers. Where else would American cigarettes come from around here?"

"And he sells them to you?"

"If I'm around. If not, I'm sure he has other contacts. His prices are good and I don't ask questions. Why should I care where they come from if the price is good?"

After he decided I had nothing to sell and wasn't interested in buying his cigarettes, fake pearls, scotch, pot, cocaine or Chinese girlfriend, he announced he had commitments that required his attention. I took the hint and took my leave.

The moon was full and the tide was ebbing. I lay on the deck of my little boat reading in the light of the bright night. Several moorage men were taking advantage of the cool illuminated hours to work on boats they were building on the nearby strand of exposed reef. I could see Masa chopping away at a big log that would become the hull of a boat. I closed my book and decided to visit him.

It never ceased to amaze me how Sama Dilaut boat builders could fashion unremarkable-looking logs into the beautiful vessels that became their homes. Most of them relied on large logs found at sea, escapees from Borneo lumber camps, for the hulls of their bigger boats. For the other parts, they trekked into the island interiors for suitable trees which they cut into planks and boards. Masa was currently completing a hull from a log he found at sea. He saw me approaching, stopped work, and leaned on his axe.

"It looks like you've almost finished the hull," I said, examining his workmanship.

"As far as I can go now. I need some planks for the sides. Tomorrow I'll go into the forest with Biti and find some trees."

"Can I come with you?" I asked. I'd never accompanied the Sama Dilaut to the forest for trees and was curious to observe the procedure.

"If you wish. We'll leave after breakfast and probably be gone two or three days."

"Great. I'll meet you in the morning." I waded back to my boat, crawled inside, recorded some thoughts in my journal, and fell asleep to the gentle moorage swells as the huge moon moved across the sky.

At sunrise, I joined Masa, his brother-in-law Biti, and their two teenage sons in their boat at the edge of the moorage. Old Laka,

Masa's mother-in-law, was also on board. We entered the strong tidal current, hoisted our sail and caught the morning breeze. It was a gorgeous clear morning. Masa handled the sail and Biti sat at the back with the steering paddle guiding us along the Tawi-Tawi coast. The boys napped on the deck, resuming sleep the early departure deprived them, while Laka fussed in the cooking area. About two hours later we reached the mouth of the Malum River. Our destination was a large stand of trees upriver beyond the Mañales house. The tide was high so we didn't have to contend with the river current until we passed the house. Then we lowered the sail and manned paddles. A half-hour later we moored at a little beach where the river broadened.

I stepped overboard into the shallow water and helped Masa secure the boat to a nearby tree. He and Biti pulled tools from under the deck. Laka handed the boys a packet of fish and cassava for our lunch and remained at the boat while the rest of us followed a path leading into the forest.

The forest was a different world from the sea world of the Sama Dilaut. We passed a few cultivated plots of cassava and bananas, but for the most part the forest was undisturbed. Biti spied a tree that would provide the planks we sought. We left the path, cut through a patch of undergrowth, and examined the tree. After deciding it was suitable, Masa and Biti stood on opposite sides of the trunk and began chopping with their axes until the tree fell. After clearing the trunk of limbs, they cut a single seam the length of either side and split the trunk into halves. We secured ropes to one of the halves and dragged the heavy log down the path toward the boat.

We reached the boat as the sun was becoming a sunset. Laka prepared dried fish and cassava and we ate in the final rays of the distant sun. We found places for sleep in the boat and slept until awakened by a morning that was still cool. We hiked to the forest to retrieve the other half of the tree and were back at the boat with it before noon. We ate a quick meal with Laka and returned to the forest where we found another tree. By late afternoon we had both halves of it at the boat. While Masa and the boys secured them for towing back to the moorage, Biti and I walked to the felling site to retrieve some of the smaller limbs. When we returned, Ramon Mañales was in animated conversation with Masa. Two armed PC officers accompanied him.

"Hello," I said. "We meet again."

"Yes," he said, obviously not pleased to see me. "I'm surprised to see you here."

"He's telling me I owe a hundred pesos for taking trees from the forest without a permit," Masa told me in Sinama. "It's too much." He handed me a slip of paper.

"These people are always taking trees without permission," said Mañales. "What is he saying? I don't speak their language."

I looked at the slip Masa gave me. It was a fine of ten pesos for cutting trees without a permit signed by Mañales.

I spoke to Masa in Sinama. "But this slip says you owe only ten pesos."

"He's trying to get a hundred pesos from me. He knows I can't read."

I turned to Mañales. "My friend says you want a hundred pesos from him, but this slip says only ten pesos."

"He's mistaken," said Mañales. "Of course, it's only ten pesos. He didn't understand me. That's the problem with these ignorant sea gypsies. They don't know Tagalog or English."

I told Masa, "He says he only asked for ten pesos."

"He's a liar. He tried to get a hundred pesos from me."

"Do you have ten pesos? Give it to him and he'll go." Masa went to the boat.

I turned to Mañales and said in English. "He misunderstood. He thought you said a hundred pesos. That would be a huge fine."

"Indeed it would," Mañales laughed.

Masa returned and handed Mañales a ten-peso bill. He looked at Masa none too happily and stuffed it in his pocket. He and his men returned to their small speedboat and sped down the river.

"He wanted a hundred pesos," said Masa. "And if you hadn't come, he would have made me pay—or beat me. I know his tactics. He does it all the time. He knows we cannot read. He writes the correct amount on the receipt and then insists we pay him a larger amount. Let's go. I don't like this place. We've been away from the sea too long."

Several days later I was in Bongao picking up my mail. I was reading a letter when I left the post office and bumped into a man who was entering. I glanced up briefly and excused myself.

"Good morning," said the man. I looked at him more closely and recognized him as one of the young PC officers with Mañales when he tried to overcharge Masa. "How are you today?"

"Fine," I said. He looked uncomfortable, smiled, and went into the post office. I sat on the bench and read my mail.

Minutes later the PC officer came out and sat beside me. "I'm sorry about last week," he said.

"What do you mean?"

He paused. He was embarrassed. "When you were in the forest with the sea gypsies. About the fine."

"Captain Mañales said it was a mistake," I said, baiting him.

"It wasn't a mistake. He does that all the time. He knows these people cannot read so he charges them exorbitant fees and then writes the correct amount on the receipt which he turns in to the Bureau of Forestry. I want you to know that some of us know what he's doing and we don't approve."

"So why don't you report him to his superiors?"

"It's not that easy. He has contacts in high places. We might lose our jobs or get demoted. He's a very corrupt man, but not all of us are like him."

"I'm sure that's true," I said. "But surely he can be reported. Maybe you could do it anonymously."

"Nothing would happen. He knows too many important people. And he has important relatives."

"He certainly gives the Philippine Constabulary a bad name."

"Yes, I know."

"Did he ever find out where the dead monkey came from that appeared on the deck when I was staying there?"

"No, and it's bothering him. Several days after you left, we found a big dead lizard with a noose around its neck in the same place. That is a bad house. All those dead animals inside. None of us like being there."

"Any clue as to who's leaving the dead animals?"

"No. But he thinks one of us is doing it."

"And what do you think?"

"I don't know," he said, after a pause. "I really don't know. Many people dislike him. He's done many bad things. Many you do not know about." He stood to leave. "I'm sorry about what happened in the forest and I wanted to tell you that I don't approve of Captain Mañales. We're not all bad."

I stood also. "Thanks for telling me," I said. "You're a good man and I wish you well." We parted.

Translation can be one of the most tedious tasks in the world. At least that was the case with the kind of translation I was doing. I'd spent most of the day with Nilan, my young research assistant, and an elderly shaman who allowed me to record his two-hour *kata-kata*, one of the sacred chants used in Sama Dilaut curing ceremonies. I recorded the chant a week previously and was now translating it. Father Raquet had loaned us a room in his school currently closed for vacation.

We'd already transcribed the chant from the tape onto paper and were now translating it from Sinama into English. It sounds like a relatively easy job, but not so. I had a battery-powered tape recorder that consumed batteries like a whale consumes plankton. Invariably, the Bongao shops were out of batteries when I needed them most. The chants themselves presented problems. They contained many obscure place names as well as "words of the ancestors," most of which were no longer understood by the chanter. After five hours, with a short break for lunch, the three of us were thoroughly exhausted and decided to call it a day. I bid the old shaman goodbye and Nilan and I walked down Bongao's only street toward the wharf where my boat was moored.

When we approached Santiago's refreshment parlor, I suggested we stop for a Coke before going to Sanga-Sanga where I would drop off Nilan and continue on to the moorage where I was currently staying. The place was crowded, but we found a window table where we could watch the always busy wharf.

"We should be able to finish the translation tomorrow," said Nilan, taking a swig of his Coke.

"I hope so. I'm tired of it. Not one of my favorite things to do."

"Hey Americano!"

I was the only American in the place so I turned toward the voice. Ramon Mañales was seated across the room with two other PCs at a table filled with beer bottles. They were dressed in military fatigues, their rifles leaned against the wall. Mañales's flushed face and watery eyes suggested he'd been drinking for some time.

I waved at him and said, "How are you?"

"Come and join us."

"We just stopped by for a quick Coke," I said, none too enthusiastic about joining three tipsy PCs with guns.

Mañales stood and walked toward us with a narrow parcel about three feet long wrapped in a dark cloth.

"I have something to show you," he said. He slapped the parcel on our table. "You're an anthropologist. I want your opinion on this."

"What is it?"

He unwrapped the parcel. "It's a kris." He pulled the blade from the scabbard and placed it on the table.

I'm no expert on krisses, but I'd seen enough of them to recognize this one as an exquisite work of art—as well as a lethal weapon. The long wavy blade was engraved with intricate curvilinear designs. Gold wire encased the handle and secured several large pearls. The silver scabbard was inscribed with Arabic script.

"This is a beautiful kris," I said. "Where did you get it?"

"I bought it from a Moro."

"Someone from here?"

"Maybe," he said. "He was at the market."

"Do you collect krisses? I saw several in your home when I was there."

"Yes, I collect them. And sell them. Let me know if you meet someone who wants one. These are authentic krisses, not the tourist junk you find in Jolo and Zamboanga. Come over and join us for a drink."

"I'm sorry but I really don't have time," I lied. I was in no rush to get back to Sanga-Sanga, but I had no interest in drinking with Mañales. "I've got to take Nilan home. Maybe another time."

He looked none too pleased at my refusal, picked up the kris, and returned to his table. Nilan and I drained our Cokes and left.

Outside, I said to Nilan, "What did you think of that kris?"

"It's a very special kris. And very old." He paused. "No one would sell a kris like that."

"Why not?"

"It's too sacred. A kris like that is from the ancestors. It's been in the family a long, long time. It has a name and many stories about its history—the battles it fought, the men it killed, the women it won. Selling it would affront the ancestors. It is sacred and no Muslim would ever let it leave the family."

"How do you suppose Mañales acquired it?"

"I don't know," said Nilan, thoughtfully. "Maybe he stole it. Maybe he killed for it. Maybe he blackmailed someone for it. He's an evil man. He kills and stuffs animals. He steals from graves. Everyone knows about him."

The exposed reef lay gasping in the midday sun, sprawling away from me in all directions. Half-plant, half-animal creatures lay exposed, seemingly struggling for their lives but in reality basking in the out-of-water stage of their amphibious life cycle. Seaweeds shriveled. It was as if someone pulled the plug of a huge bathtub and revealed its sediments to a broiling world. The tide would return in a few hours and cover everything, but now the reef was an underbelly best left hidden by the sea.

I was on a fishing trip with Masa and his extended family on the great Bilatan reef of central Tawi-Tawi. While the men fished during the day, women, children and the elderly wandered the exposed reef, collecting shells, sea slugs, seaweed, small fish, and anything else edible or sellable. It was an extremely low tide and the reef water was only ankle-deep. I'd wandered many such reefs alone, exploring the tidal pools and detritus of the bared coral but this time, I was with others, asking questions, writing notes, and taking photos.

It was not a successful trip. Windy, rainy weather prevented fishing that was normally lucrative at this time of the month. A flu bug put two adults and a boy out of commission for several days, and to top it off, one of the smaller fishing boats unmoored during the night and drifted away. Old Laka decided the ancestral spirits were unhappy about something and a trip to their graves with offerings might break our string of bad luck. Early the next morning, our little flotilla set off for the nearby cemetery island of Bunabuna'an. We moored in the shallow shore waters and several of us went to the cemetery while the others remained with the boats.

Laka approached the grave of her maternal grandmother with her bag of ritual paraphernalia. She placed lighted incense in a half-coconut shell and circled the grave with it, calling to the spirit. The rest of us were instructed to sit on the ground in a half-circle before the grave as she addressed the spirit, flattering it and requesting good fortune for all of us. She placed a cud of betel on the grave and after a brief final prayer, announced the ceremony was over. She paused and peered into the interior of the little grave house.

"Her grave marker is gone," she noted. "No wonder she's angry. Someone has taken her grave marker."

"Yes," said Masa. "It was gone when we buried Matalaini. Several other gravemarkers are gone also."

"Why didn't you tell me?" Laka asked, angrily. "This is very bad. Who has taken them?"

"The PC have them," said Masa. He looked at me. "You said you saw them at his house."

Laka turned to me, "Is that true?"

"I saw some gravemarkers at his house. I don't know if they're from here."

"Where else would they be from?" Laka asked, sharply. "Gravemarkers are gone from here and he has gravemarkers in his house."

I acknowledged that most likely she was right.

"They must be returned," she said. "The ancestors won't be content until the gravemarkers are returned. We'll stop and get them when we go back to Bongao."

"But the PC," said Biti. "You know how they are. They have guns."

"I'm not afraid of the PC," said the old woman, defiantly. "They have stolen. We'll go to them today. It's useless to waste our time fishing if the ancestors are angry."

Masa and Biti were none too enthusiastic about confronting Mañales, but Laka was adamant. Masa asked if I would accompany them, thinking Mañales would be on better behavior in my presence. I said I would.

We returned to the boats and told the others our plan to visit the PC. We lifted anchors, poled the boats to the edge of the reef, and unfurled sails. We reached the mouth of the Malum River at sunset and anchored offshore for the night.

In the early morning after a hasty breakfast, Masa, Biti, Laka and I headed upriver in one of the boats while the others remained at the anchorage. No wind inflated our sail so we paddled the heavy boat. About an hour later, our eager eyes and tired backs rounded a bend that revealed Mañales's house. We moored at the little dock and climbed the stairs to the lanai where we were met by an armed PC officer.

"What do you want?" he asked, none too cordially.

"I'd like to talk to Captain Mañales," I said.

He looked at me silently for several moments and then said, "Wait here." He walked across the lanai and entered the house. Minutes later he returned with another officer who said, "I am Captain Barata. What is your business with Captain Mañales?"

"He had some gravemarkers when I visited him here. I think they were taken from the cemetery of these people. They should be returned."

He looked at me and then at the others. "Captain Mañales was murdered last night. You haven't heard about it?"

Somehow I wasn't surprised. "We've heard nothing," I said. "We spent the night in our boats at the mouth of the river. What happened?" I translated for Masa and the others.

"His body was found here on the lanai at the door to the house. He was stabbed several times and his head almost severed. Was he a friend of yours?"

"Not a friend, an acquaintance." I told him how I knew Mañales.

"Do you know anything that might help us discover his murderer?"

"Probably no more than your men can tell you." I told him about the dead animal carcasses that were left at the door, especially the monkey dressed in fatigues with a slit throat.

"Yes, I know about that."

"I think he antagonized a lot of people," I said.

The captain didn't respond, but his expression suggested this was not news to him.

"Can we look at the gravemarkers? They should be returned to the cemetery. They're very sacred to these people."

"Do you remember where they were?"

"In the front room. In the back corner."

"Follow me," he said. We followed him into the room. The gravemarkers were still there. So were the stuffed animals. Laka looked at the markers and immediately told me they were from Bunabuna'an.

"She tells me they are the ones missing from the cemetery," I said to the captain.

He spoke to the guards in Tagalog and turned to me, "They know nothing about them. If they belong to these people, they should be returned. You can take them."

"Thank you," I said. I glanced at the wall and noticed the krisses were gone. "Do you know what happened to the krisses that were on the wall?"

"I know nothing about them. This morning was my first time to visit this house. You may take the gravemarkers. Is there anything else?" He was obviously eager for us to leave.

"No," I said. Masa, Biti, and I each picked up a grave marker and Laka led us from the house. A guard accompanied us. We climbed down the stairs to the dock and placed the markers in the boat. We paddled to the middle of the river where the current carried us downstream.

After several minutes of collective reflective silence, I asked, "Who do you think killed him?"

"Probably the families he stole the krisses from," said Masa. "Or maybe the smugglers whose cigarettes he took."

"Maybe his own men," suggested Biti.

"The ancestors killed him," said Laka, unequivocally.

Two nights later Captain Mañales's compound was destroyed by a fire of indeterminate origin. His murderer was never discovered, or perhaps more accurately, his murderer was never revealed.

The German and the Jew

t was early afternoon when we sailed into Tungkalang, the Sama Dilaut moorage across the channel from Bongao. I'd been away several days on a fishing trip with Masa's extended family. We spent a week on the sprawling reefs of central Tawi-Tawi which in those days supported a fish population that would feed half the world. We caught a healthy portion of that population and our boats were laden with dried fish and our bellies filled with fresh ones. We caught a strong wind and a favorable current at dawn that moved us over reefs and past islands, returning us home earlier than we anticipated.

When we entered the moorage, I spotted Father Raquet's little speedboat tied to the recently constructed one-room schoolhouse that served the students who sometimes attended it. Father Raquet was determined to teach Sama Dilaut children the basics of literacy, although it sometimes seemed hopeless since most of them were in the moorage only a few days or weeks at a time before taking off with their families for distant fishing grounds. The school was taught by a land-dwelling Muslim woman and Father Raquet visited periodically to check its progress. After transferring the dried fish stowed in my boat to Masa's boat, I paddled to the school where Father sat on the deck with a Caucasian man.

"I was hoping I'd find you here," he said. "Toss me your rope." I threw my mooring rope to him and climbed the ladder to the deck.

"We have a visitor," he said. "This is Karl . . . I'm sorry but I forgot your last name."

"Schlimmermann," said the man. His multi-syllabic utterance revealed a heavy Teutonic accent.

"This is our resident anthropologist I was telling you about," said Father. I clasped the man's extended hand.

You could tell he was German a mile away, probably what Hitler had in mind for his super race of Aryans. Over six feet tall and deeply tanned by his tropical travels, he was blond with green eyes and a wide mouth filled with strong white teeth. His T-shirt and shorts showed off a lean, muscular body. He flashed a generous smile at me. Karl Schlimmermann was a very good-looking man, but his looks were too perfect for my taste. I like a few flaws in my beauty.

"Karl's traveling throughout the Philippines and writing a book. He wants to get a first-hand look at the Sama Dilaut and he will be sleeping in the schoolhouse for a couple of nights."

"And I greatly appreciate it," said the German.

"What part of Germany are you from?" I asked.

He smiled. "You recognized my accent. I'm German by birth, but I live in Australia now. Sydney."

Father interjected, "Karl plans to include a chapter about the Sama Dilaut in his book."

"I'm interested in hearing about your research."

"I'm always ready to talk about that," I laughed. "Ask Father. I tell him more than he wants to know about the Sama Dilaut."

"Never," said Father Raquet, "but I must get back to Bongao before the retreating tide traps me." He pulled his boat to the deck and stepped into it. "Enjoy your visit," he said to Karl.

"I will. And thanks for your hospitality."

"My pleasure," said Father Raquet. After several attempts, his motor started and we watched him wend through the moorage toward the open channel.

The tide was rapidly retreating and several moorage children waded toward us to check out Karl. Visitors like him were rare in Tawi-Tawi. The occasional American or European wandered through but for the most part Tawi-Tawi was off the beaten track. About a month earlier, an overbearing American arrived expecting me to accommodate him as he "experienced" the Sama Dilaut. After three days, I grew tired of feeding him and suggested it was time for him to move on. A couple others had made brief appearances and overall I was unimpressed. The German seemed different.

"The tide's low enough now to walk around the moorage," I said. "I'll introduce you to the headman."

"Thanks. That would be great."

We climbed down the ladder into the foot-deep water and made our way toward the houseboat of the headman. He was a pleasant old man and welcomed Karl to the moorage. He insisted we accept a gift of tuna for dinner. We happily did so and headed back toward the schoolhouse. The sun was slipping well into the west and we were both ready for something to eat. We cooked the fish and some rice in my boat and ate on the deck of the schoolhouse in the setting sun. Afterward we stretched out and watched the stars emerge, trying to identify constellations.

"When did you leave Germany?" I asked.

"As soon as I could after the war."

"Where were you during the war?"

"Munich most of the time, but I was drafted into the army the last year. I was only fifteen. My parents hated Hitler and his war. I hated him too. Not exactly the best mindset for fighting his cause."

He lit a cigarette.

"I can well imagine," I said. "Did you make it to a combat zone?"

"I was at the Battle of the Bulge."

"That must've been brutal. And in the dead of winter too."

"That's when I decided if I survived the war, I'd leave Germany and live someplace where it's always warm. I left as soon as I could. My parents were both killed in the war. Only my brother was left and we were never close. I went to Australia in 1946 with a group of Jews. I've never returned to Germany and probably never will."

"How did you end up with a group of Jews?"

"Pure chance. It was during the chaos after surrender. There was no food anywhere. I left my unit and got rid of my uniform as soon as possible. I was young and no one suspected I'd been a soldier. I wandered several months doing anything to survive. In the fall of 1945, I hitched a train to Munich. I saw a center where Jews from the camps were sheltered until it was decided what to do with them. I met a guy about my age who told me he was living in the camp and passing as a Jew so he'd have a place to stay and something to eat. I joined him."

"You don't exactly look like a Jew."

"You're thinking in stereotypes. A lot of German Jews don't look like Jews. They're the ones who escaped the camps. I heard that Jews were being transported to the United States and Australia so I continued the charade and ended up in Australia."

"So you have the Jews to thank for Australia?"

"I owe the Jews nothing," he said icily. "They were responsible for the war."

That one took me by surprise. A long silence followed. Finally, I said, "How can you possibly blame the Jews for the war?"

"If they didn't have their claws on everything, Germany wouldn't have been in such bad shape and Hitler would never have gained power."

I was no expert on German history, but this seemed a rather perverted interpretation of events. "Even if that were true, do you think that justifies what Hitler did to them?"

"Of course not. I'm not saying they deserved the death camps, but they brought on what happened to them."

"It would be difficult for me to disagree with you more."

He was silent for several moments. "Are you a Jew?"

"No, but two branches of my family are."

"Maybe we'd better talk about something else."

"I think that's a good idea."

A long silence followed as we both tried to think of something harmless to talk about. I dislike bigots of every stripe, but it looked like I was stuck with this guy for a couple of days. So I did what I usually do when I'm stuck with such people. I directed the conversation to something that interested me. I asked him about his travels.

He'd been in places where I'd traveled and we talked about our experiences. He was no dummy and had done a lot of reading about the Philippines and Indonesia before he set out on his trip. Despite his views on Jews, he had a good sense of

cultural relativity and lacked the ethnocentrism that perverts
many casual travelers. He'd been on the road about four
months and planned to be out another two before returning
to Sydney where he would write his book.

It was getting late and the moorage was tucked in for
the night. We decided to do the same. Karl went into the
schoolhouse and by the light of a weak kerosene lamp rolled
out his sleeping bag. I returned to my boat, stretched out on
its narrow deck and looked up at the stars until the gentle
swells of the moorage rocked me to sleep.

The next morning Karl and I ate breakfast from some of the
cans he brought with him. Following our tinny repast, we
walked around the moorage. I introduced him to some of
my friends and then left him on his own with his camera.
He was wading toward Sanga–Sanga Island when I last saw
him.

I returned to my boat and reread my notes about
Sama Dilaut religion which simplistically could be called
"ancestor worship" but in reality is much more complex.
I was beginning to understand its general outlines, and
was now interviewing shamans to gain an appreciation
of its idiosyncrasies. I waded to the houseboat of Laka, an
important shaman in the moorage.

"Who's your friend?" she asked as I approached her houseboat. She was sitting at the stern feeding wood to a fire that boiled a pot of fish.

"A visitor," I said.

"Tell him he can sleep in my boat if he gets lonely tonight," she laughed. "We old women are better." Laka enjoyed joking about her libido.

"I'll give him the word. Do you have time to talk?"

"What do you want this time? I'm busy but I suppose I can talk while I'm working. Get out your paper and pencil. Do you want to take pictures? Where's your camera?" By now, Laka knew my routine. She always gave me a tough time, but she was in fact one of my most important contacts for understanding her culture. And one of my best friends among the Sama Dilaut.

"I want to know more about the *saitan*," I said, sitting on the edge of her houseboat. The *saitan* were spirits that shamans sometimes contacted in their healing ceremonies.

"Them," she said disgustedly, spitting a mouthful of betel juice over the side of the boat. "I wish they'd leave me alone. I'm getting too old for them." She was referring to the possession she sometimes experienced when the *saitan* visited her.

"How old were you when the *saitan* first came to you?"

"After my mother died," she said, looking toward an approaching motorboat.

I followed her glance and saw Father Raquet's boat winding through the houseboats toward the schoolhouse. He was not alone. A Caucasian woman was with him.

"I better go see what he wants," I said.

"You can't fool me," laughed Laka. "You want to check out that woman. I told you we old women are better."

"Promises, promises. Always teasing, but never any action."

"One of these days I'll surprise you. Here's some fish. Maybe if you feed her, she'll be good to you."

I thanked her for the string of fish and waded toward the schoolhouse.

Father Raquet waved at my approach. "I've brought another visitor," he said.

"Always happy to have company," I responded as I caught Father's mooring rope and secured it to one of the piles of the schoolhouse. He and the woman climbed up the ladder to the deck. I followed them.

"I'm Rachel Robanan," the woman announced before Father Raquet could introduce us. She was attractive, tall and slim, with short dark hair and olive skin, probably in her mid-twenties. I didn't recognize her accent. She could've hailed from anywhere around the Mediterranean or perhaps the Middle East.

"What brings you to Tawi-Tawi?" I asked her.

"Mostly curiosity. I've always been attracted to tropical islands and there seems an abundance of them down here."

"Rachel is a schoolteacher from Israel," explained Father Raquet. "She wants to visit my school and learn about my efforts to coax Sama Dilaut children into the classroom."

"What grade level do you teach?" I asked.

"Actually I don't teach anymore. I work in the curriculum division of the Israeli government. I'm mostly involved in developing curricula for elementary schools, especially for recently arrived immigrant children."

"Sounds sort of anthropological."

"Yes, it is. I'm on sabbatical leave and part of that includes visiting schools relevant to my job. I couldn't resist coming here after learning about Father Raquet's school. I'm also down here to see Muslim culture first-hand. As an Israeli, it's impossible for me to visit Muslim countries, so I'm visiting the Muslim provinces here in the Philippines."

By now the deck was crowded with smiling, curious children. For many of them, Rachel was probably the first white woman they'd seen. They stared at her unabashed.

"Is Karl around?" asked Father Raquet.

"Not at the moment. He was wandering around the moorage earlier, but I think he went to the island to check out the land village. I'm not sure when he'll be back."

"We have a minor problem. After no visitors for many months, we have two who are interested in staying in the moorage. Rachel would like to meet our teacher tomorrow and spend a couple of days observing the classroom. She'll need to sleep here in the school. Do you know how long Karl plans to stay?"

"I think he's leaving tomorrow."

"Is there somewhere he could stay tonight so Rachel can sleep in the school?"

I knew he was suggesting that Karl sleep in my boat. I wasn't crazy about hosting two visitors, let alone one of them sleeping with me. But I was a visitor myself and Father had been good to me, so it was time for some reciprocation.

"I'm sorry to intrude," said Rachel. "But I only have three days here and I'd like to include this school in my sabbatical report."

"No problem. Karl can sleep in my boat."

We entered the school and Father Raquet showed its meager furnishings to Rachel. It was one-room with a blackboard at the front and a small kitchenette with a two-burner kerosene stove in a back corner. Mismatched chairs and desks were scattered about. A few very used books were piled on a makeshift table in a corner.

"I'm afraid it's not much of a school," said Father. "We're operating on a very small budget. Mrs. Usman comes four days a week and teaches whatever children show up. Most families follow the fishing cycles and consequently are never here very long."

Rachel asked questions about curricula and some of the special problems of the school. She quizzed me about the Sama

Dilaut, and before long we'd devoured an hour and it was mid-afternoon.

"I must return to Bongao," said Father. "I'm sorry there's no bed here, but perhaps you can spread your sleeping bag on the table. If you want to cook you can use the kitchen."

"I brought canned food. I'll be fine."

"I've written a note to Mrs. Usman explaining your interest. You can give it to her when she arrives tomorrow. I think you'll get on well with her."

"I can't tell you how much I appreciate your kindness in letting me stay here," said Rachel. "I'll make a contribution to your school when I leave."

"That's very kind of you."

We went onto the deck and Father Raquet climbed down to his speedboat. He engaged the motor and we watched him slowly maneuver through the houseboats to the channel where he opened the throttle and sped toward Bongao.

"The tide's too high to show you the moorage today, but it'll be out in the morning. I'll give you a tour and introduce you to some people."

"I would appreciate that."

"Were you born in Israel?"

"No. Berlin. My parents were able to get me out but they were there during the war."

"They survived the war?"

"Yes, but with many scars. They were at Auschwitz. They both died the year after I finished college. From ailments stemming from Auschwitz."

We silently watched four boys floating toy boats in the moorage waters.

"Have you visited Germany since the war?" I asked.

"No. Never. And I never will. I hate Germany and detest Germans."

I was taken aback by her vehemence. After a short silence, I said, "I can understand your feelings."

She looked at me. "Thank you, but I doubt if you can really understand my feelings."

"Probably not," I agreed.

"I'm currently involved in an oral history project collecting stories from Holocaust survivors. I had no love for Germans when I began the project. My contempt for them now is beyond measure."

"But surely you don't blame all Germans for what happened to the Jews."

"I do. Obviously not the children. But every adult German must assume some responsibility for the murder of the Jews. They allowed it to happen."

We continued watching the children play in the water.

"I think I should tell you," I began. "The man staying here is a German—from Australia."

"Was he born in Australia?"

"No. Germany. He was only a teenager when he was drafted into the army. He left Germany after the war."

She was silent. "I'll be civil to him. There's no need for me to spend time with him. You said he's leaving tomorrow?"

"Yes."

"You probably think I'm an intolerant bigot."

After a small silence, I said, "I can understand your anger. But I can't appreciate your condemnation of all Germans."

"No, I'm sure you can't." She then asked, obviously changing the subject, "How many people live at this moorage?"

"It varies tremendously. During the dark moon when ceremonies are held and people rest from fishing, sometimes more than a hundred houseboats are here. But at other times when everyone's out fishing, no more than a couple dozen." I glanced across the moorage. "Here comes Karl now. It looks like he got caught in the rising tide."

Karl was wading among the houseboats through waist-deep water holding his clothes and camera above his head. "I forgot about the changing tide," he yelled when he saw us watching him. "I almost got stranded on the island."

"Sorry," I said. "I forgot to warn you."

He climbed up the ladder to the deck, wearing only his underwear and revealing a trim muscular well-endowed body. Rachel looked at him appraisingly. "Sorry," he said, smiling at her. "Let me get decent." He held his clothes in front of him and disappeared into the schoolhouse. A few minutes later, he emerged in shorts and T-shirt. He sat on the deck beside us and I introduced him to Rachel.

"Rachel's visiting the school for a couple of days," I explained. "If you don't mind sleeping in my boat, she'll sleep in the schoolhouse tonight."

"Not a problem. I wondered what it would be like sleeping in one of these houseboats. Now I have a chance to find out." He turned to Rachel and asked, "Where are you from?"

"Israel," she said, looking at him steadily. "And you?"

"I'm Australian."

"Your accent tells me you were somewhere else before Australia."

"I was born in Germany. I left when I was very young."

"How young?"

"Fifteen. Were you born in Israel?"

"No, Berlin. My parents got me out, but they weren't so lucky. They were at Auschwitz."

There was an awkward pause.

"I'm sorry," Karl said.

"I hear that a lot from Germans," Rachel said icily. "Had they done something during the war, they wouldn't need to be so sorry now." She looked at Karl steadily.

He returned her look and said, "Maybe it wasn't entirely their fault."

"Please. Don't tell me the Jews brought it on themselves."

"They must've done something to anger the Germans so much."

"Sure. Like by being Jews?"

I interrupted. "This conversation is not going in a good direction. World War II ended eighteen years ago. Let's talk about something else." I turned to Karl, "Tell me more about the book you're working on. Will it be mostly photos?"

He was happy to change the subject. "A lot of photos, but a lot of text too. I want to include ethnographic information about the people I visit, but also some personal sketches. For example, I'll have a section about the Sama Dilaut, but also something about you and Father Raquet. Maybe Rachel too."

She smiled at him for the first time.

I asked him about the ethnic groups he'd already visited. He'd obviously done a lot of research before he left Australia and had a clear idea of what he wanted the book to be. It seemed several cuts above most travel books. He talked about his travels. Rachel and I had visited some of the places and added our travel tales. Then we paused to watch a fiery display of reds in the west conclude the day.

"Anyone hungry?" I asked.

"Starving," said Rachel. "Isn't there a kitchen of sorts in the school?"

"'Of sorts' is right. A two-burner kerosene stove. I have some fish and we can cook some rice. Maybe some of your cans can complete the menu. I'll get the stove started and you can cook the rice while I clean the fish."

We went inside and I lighted the stove. I showed them the rice, pans, and water, and returned to the deck and cleaned the fish Laka gave me. Several minutes later, Karl came out. "Can you believe it," he said "neither of us packed a can-opener. Do you have one?"

"There's one in the boat. I'll get it after I finish these fish."

"She's a beautiful woman, isn't she? Too bad she hates me."

"You didn't exactly help matters with your twisted interpretation of Jewish blame for the Holocaust."

"I tell it like I see it."

"And therefore suffer the consequences."

I went to my boat, found a rusty can-opener, and gave it to Karl. I tossed the fish into a pan of water and boiled them with some chili peppers and soy sauce. When everything was cooked, we scooped the food onto chipped plates and carried them to the deck where we ate and watched the darkening moorage.

I steered the conversation to harmless subjects. I asked Rachel about her work with refugee children and the cross-cultural challenges involved in developing school curricula for them. At my probing, Karl discussed photography and how he captured and created what he wanted on film. I was genuinely interested in their work, Rachel because some anthropology was obviously important in what she was doing, and Karl because I wanted to improve my amateur photography.

We laughed at one another's travel stories and reminisced about what we missed from home. Each time it appeared that things were warming between Karl and Rachel, a chill crept in to remind me otherwise. Beneath the chill, however, I sensed a mutual physical attraction, but it seemed unable to bridge the emotional chasm separating them. I felt like an intruder into the maelstrom of emotions flooding the deck.

Eventually our conversation waned and we lay back entertaining private thoughts and gazing up at the starry sky. I began dozing and decided it was time to retire.

"Bedtime for me," I announced.

"Me too," said Rachel, standing.

"I'll get my backpack from the school," said Karl. "I left it in the corner."

He went into the schoolhouse and Rachel followed with a small flashlight she produced from her pocket. I went to the stairs leading to the water and pulled my boat toward me. Masa and his brother passed in their boat.

"Going fishing?" I asked.

"Yes," he replied. "You want to come?"

"Not tonight. I have visitors."

"So I noticed. Who gets the woman?" He laughed.

"It's not that way. She's on her own. If you have any luck tonight, I'll buy some of your fish for the breakfast."

"If I have any luck, I'll give you some. See you tomorrow."

They disappeared into the darkness and I waited for Karl. He finally appeared in the doorway.

"Follow me," I instructed him.

We climbed into my boat. About sixteen feet long with a keel of only about three feet, it allowed two slim people to sleep feet to feet with little wiggle room. A planked platform over the outriggers on either side provided additional space. A nipa mat served as a tent-like roof that was easily dismantled for sailing.

"If you're okay with that end, I'll take this one," I said crawling to the stern of the boat.

"I'm fine here," he said, placing his gear on the platforms on either side.

"Make sure the rope is secured to the schoolhouse. We don't want to drift away during the night."

We talked awhile and then settled down for some serious sleep. I heard his soft snore and soon added mine to the sounds of the moorage.

About a half-hour later, I awakened. Karl was at the bow quietly pulling the mooring rope. He pulled the boat to the schoolhouse and stealthily climbed the steps to the deck. He paused and looked back, apparently checking that I was sleeping. I said nothing. The moonlight illuminated the deck and I saw him slip into the schoolhouse.

I waited for whatever might follow. Boards creaked as he walked across the room. Then I heard his weight settle onto the floor. He and Rachel exchanged muffled words I couldn't understand. I heard more creaking boards and then the unmistakable sounds of sex.

"I'll be damned," I mumbled to myself. I rolled over and drifted back to sleep. Some time later, I awakened. Things were still happening in the schoolhouse.

I awoke again when Karl returned to the boat. I feigned sleep.

When I awakened the sun was beyond sunrise and Karl was snoring at his end of the boat. I lay quietly as sleep retreated from my head. Karl began to stir. He sat up.

"Good morning," I said. "Did you sleep well?"

"Like a baby. This boat rocks like a cradle." He looked at the water. "The tide is low."

"Yes. It went out during the night."

"I'm going to wade to the island while it's out. I want to get some more photos." He packed his possessions into his backpack.

"Don't you want some breakfast? We can rustle something up among the three of us."

"No. I've got some food in my backpack. I'll eat later." He obviously was eager to be on his way. "I probably won't see you before I fly out this afternoon. I really appreciate your hospitality. Give me an address and I'll send you a copy of my book when it's published."

"I'd like that." I found a slip of paper and wrote an address on it. He handed me a card with his address. He put on his flip-flops and slipped over the side of the boat into the knee-deep water.

"Don't you want to say goodbye to Rachel?"

"Not particularly."

He turned and waded toward the island. I wasn't unhappy to see him go. I crawled to the bow and pulled the boat to the schoolhouse steps. I heard Rachel stirring within. I climbed to the deck as she appeared at the door.

"Care for a cup of coffee?" she asked.

"I'd love it. Karl has left already."

She looked at the clear sky, yawned, stretched her arms upward and said, "I wondered why the air seemed so clean this morning. I'll get your coffee."

She turned and entered the schoolhouse.

Nilan and Nalana

Everyone who visits Tawi-Tawi thinks about climbing Mount Bongao, and a few of them actually do it. The mountain is the most prominent peak in the province, rising dramatically and abruptly from the sea and then gradually returning to it on the opposite side. According to local lore, two graves at its summit are the resting places of the earliest Muslim missionaries in Tawi-Tawi and consequently are extremely sacred to the local people. But long before Islam came to Tawi-Tawi, the mountaintop was probably already a sacred site. Its startling presence most likely attracted the spiritual attention of the earliest human inhabitants of the islands.

I wanted to climb Mount Bongao the day I saw it, but it took a while before that happened. Today was the day. I was on a pilgrimage to the graves with Masa, Laka, and Nilan, my young research assistant and sometimes interpreter. Several weeks previously, Masa's wife was seriously ill and during her healing ceremonies, Masa promised he would visit the graves if the spirits permitted her recovery. She recovered and today we awakened at dawn, ate a big breakfast, and paddled across the channel to Bongao Island to fulfill the promise.

We moored our boat, crossed the wide sandy beach, and approached the forest at the base of the mountain. Laka stopped and announced that we must hold a ceremony for the mountain spirits to ensure a safe climb. We sat in a small circle while she lighted incense, fanning the flame until its embers emitted a column of smoke to attract the spirits. She uttered a prayer and asked the spirits to protect us as we climbed the mountain. She then doused the incense and told us we could now safely ascend the mountain.

She led us up a worn trail, stopping occasionally, and knotting long blades of grass that grew along the way. "For the spirits," she told me, knowing I had questions about everything and understood nothing. About ten minutes later, she stopped again and said we must maintain silence until she instructed us otherwise. We passed through dense forest and the slippery, rock-strewn trail demanded our full attention. About two-thirds up the mountain, she called our attention to a clearing filled with small green and white flags, offerings to the spirits. She pulled two small flags, one white and one green, from her bag and added them to the collection.

After another steep slippery climb, we emerged on a grassy plain at the summit where we were immediately surrounded by a troop of monkeys, the legendary white monkeys, guardians of Mount Bongao's sacred graves. They weren't white, but they were considerably lighter and smaller than the dark brown ones found in neighboring islands. We had bananas for them and they approached us expectantly. Laka uttered another brief prayer and instructed us to give the monkeys our bananas. They came with outstretched hands, greedily grabbing the fruit, and retreating to nearby trees.

I was considering how the many visitors to the graves probably altered the monkeys' social behavior when I heard female voices behind the shrubbery to my left. Two teenaged girls emerged followed by an old woman. The prettier of the two girls started when she saw us or more specifically when she saw Nilan.

"What a surprise," she said. "What are you doing here, Nilan?"

"We're visiting the graves. And you?" A broad smile engulfed Nilan's face. He was obviously happy to see her.

"The same. A promise to my grandmother's spirit."

"Are you ready for the beginning of school?"

"Yes. Are you?"

The old woman looked uneasy and disapproving. "Come, Nalana," she said. At that moment, a middle-aged man appeared from the shrubbery. When he saw Nilan, his blank expression turned sullen. Nilan became apprehensive.

"Nalana," said the man firmly. "We must go. Come immediately."

She looked at Nilan with an expression of resignation and followed the man and the other women. They disappeared down the path.

"Who was that?" I asked.

"His name is Hajji Yusup," said Nilan.

"I mean the girl."

He was momentarily silent and then said, "A classmate from school." It was apparent that she was more than just a classmate, but before I could ask more, he joined Laka at the grave in the center of the clearing.

As Laka prepared her ritual, I took in the panoramic view. To my right stretched the long island of Tawi-Tawi flanked by dozens of small green islands and sprawling aqua reefs. Other islands spread southwestward in the opposite direction like stepping stones toward Borneo and its cloud-shrouded summits. I clicked away with my camera and then joined the others at the grave where Laka was arranging the ritual paraphernalia. We sat in a half-circle while she addressed the spirits, asking them to accept the offerings and reminding them we were fulfilling our promise. When she finished, we ate the food and drank the water while the spirits consumed the spiritual counterparts.

I wandered off with my camera to capture more of the spectacular views. When I returned to the grave, the others were waiting for me. The greedy monkeys approached for more bananas, but we had none to give.

The next day I took advantage of a brisk wind and sailed to Bongao to pick up supplies. I found all I needed at my favorite Chinese store and since it was still mid-afternoon, I decided to visit Father Raquet.

When I arrived at the convento, his old cook Tia was puttering in the kitchen. She told me Father was in his garden where I found him watering a very thirsty-looking bougainvillea.

He greeted me. "You caught me in the act. I'm murdering yet another plant."

I laughed. "It looks like a merciful death."

In the right environment, all kinds of flowers thrive throughout Tawi-Tawi. However, the land surrounding Father Raquet's convento was solid rock covered with a few inches of infertile soil. He tried growing a variety of plants without success. Even potted plants met their demise under his supervision, partly because his busy schedule often precluded watering.

"You'd think I would give up, wouldn't you?" he asked.

"Hope springs eternal in the human heart according to Alexander Pope."

"Perhaps, but Alexander Pope never tried growing flowers in my garden. Let me finish watering and we'll go to the patio. I'm ready for some shade."

I filled a bucket from a nearby rain barrel and watered a struggling palm.

"Poor things," said Father. "Perhaps it would be kinder if I let them die. Maybe I'll try cactus. But I'd probably kill them too."

"Have you considered plastic?"

He laughed. "I'm sure I'd do them in too."

I finished watering and sought the shade of the patio. Father Raquet appeared with two frosty San Miguel beers. We settled into chairs as I told him about my trek up Mount Bongao.

"I met a hajji up there. Not a very pleasant fellow. Hajji Yusup. Do you know him?"

"Yes. He's from Pagasinan. A very successful smuggler—or businessman, as he prefers to be called. He's never been unpleasant to me."

"Maybe he didn't like my company." I told him about his reaction to Nilan.

"Ah yes. That explains it. Those two families have been feuding for years."

"About what?"

"Who knows? They've probably forgotten. You've been here long enough to know how these feuds go on for generations. I think this one dates back to a dispute over land on Banaran Island. It would be laughable if so many people hadn't been killed over the years."

"Killed? Over the land?"

"Not the land, the feud. The slightest provocation reignites it."

"Has anyone ever been prosecuted for the killings?"

"Not that I know of. There are never any witnesses—at least, none came forward."

"I don't think the feud extends to Nilan and Nalana," I said. "In fact, I think they may be sweethearts."

"No wonder Hajji Yusup was angry. I've never heard of a marriage between those two families. Too bad. Maybe it would end the feud."

A week later I was at Lioboran, a Sama Dilaut moorage in central Tawi-Tawi where Nilan and I were attending a wedding. The afternoon before the ceremony, we conducted a quick census to see how many houseboats were congregated for the celebration. Now we sat in my boat on the drained reef in late-afternoon, watching the tide come in. Little gurgling rivulets overflowed tidal pools, slowly flooding the sprawling reef. Soon all would be sea again and no one would suspect a great reef lay beneath the watery surface stretching in all directions.

"Do you know the couple getting married tomorrow?" I asked Nilan as we watched fishing boats gather at the edge of the reef waiting for the waters to deepen so they could return to the moorage.

"I know the groom's family. They sometimes moor near my village. I don't know the bride's family."

"They seem rather old by Sama Dilaut standards."

He laughed. "Yes. Almost as old as I am."

"When do you plan to marry?"

"Soon, if I had my way. But not to the girls my family wants me to marry. Every month they come up with another bride for me."

"Are you picky? Or are their choices bad?"

"Both. I'm interested in only one girl." He paused. "Nalana. You saw her when we were on Mount Bongao."

"She's very pretty."

"She's the most beautiful, wonderful woman in all of Tawi-Tawi." His wide smile spread across his face. Even his ears and nose seemed to smile. "We've been in love since we were very young."

"And your family doesn't approve of her?"

"Yes." He was silent several moments. "But I think they'd consent if her father would. Hajji Yusup hates my family. He won't let Nalana talk to me."

"Why does he hate your family?" I was curious to hear his version of what Father Raquet told me.

"Because of an old feud. It was long ago. I don't even know what it was about."

"Makes it difficult to have a relationship, doesn't it?"

"We meet at school. Our friends carry messages for us. We write letters." He paused. "I'm a good man. I work hard. Soon I'll graduate from high school. I'm a devout Muslim. I'd make a good husband for Nalana, but Hajji Yusup won't even consider our marriage."

"So what are you going to do?"

"I don't know. But I can't stop loving Nalana."

We cooked our fish and cassava as darkness descended. The small kerosene lamps and cooking fires of the houseboats provided illumination on the water while overhead a sky full of stars and a bright moon added additional light. On the beach, gongs and drums summoned people to the dances that would begin the wedding celebration. We finished our meal and washed our dishes. I grabbed my notebook and camera and we paddled toward the beach.

When we returned to Bongao two days later, I gave Nilan the week off. He was beginning his final semester and busy with activities surrounding the opening of school. He worked with me in the mornings and attended classes in Bongao during the afternoon. It was now Monday morning. I sat in my houseboat watching the morning activities in the moorage and waiting for Nilan. Punctual as always, he paddled in at eight o'clock, greeted me, dismantled his sail, and looked at his watch. "Only twenty-five minutes. The wind and current were good," he said. He told me about school, obviously happy to be back with his friends. We began tabulating census data. It was tedious work and after a couple of hours, we took a break.

"Do you like your classes?" I asked, standing to stretch.

"They're okay. Nothing too great so far. But it's good to see my friends again."

"Did you see Nalana?"

"Yes. Many times." He beamed. "That's the best part of school."

"Is she in your classes?"

"Yes. We'll both graduate at the end of this term." He paused. "I told her I want to marry her and she said she wants to marry me. She thought about no one but me during semester break. And I thought only of her."

"Does her family know?"

"No." His happy mood darkened. "But I'm going to ask my family to approach her family. Nalana is her father's favorite and she thinks he'll listen to her. It's the old people who keep this feud going. We young people don't care about it."

"Will your family offer bride wealth?"

"I think so. I talked to two of my cousins. They're supportive. We'll talk to my parents and my aunts and uncles. They'd like to forget this feud, but Nalana's father is obstinate."

"That presents a serious obstacle, doesn't it?"

"I'm hoping that when he learns how much Nalana loves me, he'll change his mind."

Three weeks later I was sitting in a house in Kabukat, a village on a little island across the channel from Bongao. Nilan had talked his parents into making a formal marriage proposal to Nalana's family which included the offering of bride wealth and I was invited to attend. Curious to witness the proposal ceremony, I eagerly accepted the invitation. Nilan and his parents were absent, as were Nalana and her parents. Tradition demanded that the potential bride and groom and their parents be uninvolved in the bride wealth negotiations.

In Tawi-Tawi, bride wealth determines the status of the bride when she joins her new in-laws. Most families do not have savings to pay it when their sons marry and thus call on kinsmen to contribute. When daughters marry, the bride wealth received is redistributed to those kinsmen who helped sons marry in the past. Consequently, the tradition not only provides status to the bride, but also redistributes wealth and cements bonds of kinship. But this anthropological interpretation was not on the minds of the participants in the ceremony I was joining. They were simply following tradition.

When we arrived, Nalana's relatives cordially invited us into their home. The walls were hung with brightly colored buntings and the floor spread with the family's finest mats. The rainbow clothing of the participants added to the festive setting.

Nilan was represented by two aunts, two uncles, two cousins, and me. One of the uncles carried a small box wrapped in a bright green cloth containing jewelry and five hundred pesos. He placed the box before him and we sat on mats in a semi-circle. Opposite us completing the circle were six members of Nalana's extended family. They offered us betel and cigarettes which we accepted according to our tastes. I didn't care much for either, but refusal would be bad manners so I smoked a symbolic cigarette.

After some innocuous conversation, Nilan's uncle announced our reason for being there—as if no one knew. He explained that Nilan's family wished to offer bride wealth to Nalana's family for the marriage of the young couple. He spoke of Nilan's fine qualities, his soon-to-be completed high school degree, his devotion to Islam, and his high regard among his family, peers, and village. The litany continued. He concluded by noting that the families had their differences in the past, but it was time to forget the old feud and become friends. He was certain Allah wished them to reconcile. He then gently pushed the box to the middle of the circle.

Following a brief pause, an older man from Nalana's family said they were flattered that Nilan's family was interested in Nalana as a bride for Nilan. He accepted the box and said his family would discuss the proposal. At that point women arrived with food and Coca-Cola, the champagne of Tawi-Tawi ceremonies. The refreshments eased tensions and conversation flowed more easily. It would be several days before Nalana's family responded to the marriage proposal. Typically, they would request a higher price and Nilan's family would either accept it or offer a somewhat lower price to continue the negotiations. If Nalana's family responded with an exorbitantly high price, it signaled they were not interested in the marriage.

Suddenly a screeching roar drowned our conversations and the next moment the entire roof of the house was carried away by a violent wind that freakishly left the remaining house intact. After a moment of bewilderment, everyone stood, some crying and shouting. With others, I rushed to the deck outside and discovered all the surrounding houses intact. Neighbors were shouting and staring at our roofless house. One of them reported that a water spout approached the village, moved above it and suddenly dipped down, taking our roof and dropping it in the nearby sea. The old imam who hosted our ceremony announced that we must go to the mosque immediately and thank Allah for sparing us. They found a prayer cap for me and we hurried to the nearby mosque. The imam offered prayers to Allah and then lighted incense and thanked the ancestors. We left the mosque and lingered outside, swapping stories about the bizarre incident until someone from Nilan's family announced it was time for us to return home.

The following morning I arrived at Nilan's village. We had arranged to sail to the Bilatan reefs where we would join Masa's family in a communal fish drive, a type of Sama Dilaut fishing I'd never seen before.

"I heard about the storm," was the first thing Nilan said to me. "Thanks to Allah no one was hurt. You must've been terrified."

"It happened too quickly to be scared. And yes, thankfully no one was injured."

"Do you think Nalana's family was pleased with the offer?"

"It's difficult to know. They were very reserved. But I guess that's the way those ceremonies are."

"Yes. They would be polite. And nothing would be said about the offer."

We caught a favorable wind that hurried us to the sprawling reefs of central Tawi-Tawi. We arrived late afternoon and discovered Masa and his family near a small uninhabited island where we'd arranged to meet them. We anchored, waded ashore, and found a sheltered place to build a fire for cooking rice while Masa and his brother fished the nearby waters. We ate to a setting sun and returned to our boats for sleep.

The next day at dawn we joined about two dozen other fishermen and their boats. It was full moon, a time when huge schools of fish invaded the flooded reefs for food normally unavailable to them. Each month if the weather permitted, Sama Dilaut fishermen awaited their arrival with nets and spears. This time I joined them and for four days, we netted literally thousands of fish during the high tides and waited for their return during the low tides when we dried and salted the catches for the fish buyers in Bongao. Nilan was obviously anxious about his marriage proposal and frequently asked me if I saw any reactions among Nalana's family. I patiently repeated that I saw nothing indicating approval or disapproval.

When we awakened on the fifth day, the tide was lowering, the fish were gone and it was time to return home. We hoisted our sail and headed back toward Nilan's village where we were greeted by two teenaged boys when we moored at the pier. Nilan immediately asked them, "Is there any word from Nalana's family?"

The boys' smiles turned sober and after a long pause, one of them said, "Yes. It's not good."

"What is it?"

"The old people say the storm was a sign from Allah and the ancestors. They say it will be bad for both families and no babies will be born. They won't allow the marriage."

Nilan was silent.

"I'm sorry," I said.

"I must go to my father." Nilan jumped from the boat and ran down the pier toward the village.

I wasn't surprised when Nilan didn't show up the next day. Three days later, his cousin Basata arrived with a message from Nilan's father telling me he was concerned about Nilan and asked if I would come and talk to him. I was more than willing to oblige and returned with Basata to the little village a few miles down the coast. Nilan's parents met me on the deck of their house.

"We're worried about Nilan," said the father. "He won't talk to anyone and he won't eat. He stays in the house staring at the wall. It is not good. A shaman and an imam both prayed for him, but he's no better. You're his friend. Maybe he'll talk to you." He led me inside the house and pointed to a back corner where Nilan lay on a mat staring into the wall.

"Maybe it would be best if you left us alone," I suggested.

"Yes." He returned to the deck.

I went to Nilan and sat on the floor cross-legged beside him. "I've come to see you, Nilan."

He glanced at me and said nothing. He looked wan and unkempt, his eyes red-rimmed and his hair uncombed.

I reached over and placed my hand on his shoulder. "What is it, Nilan? You can tell me."

He looked at me blankly and then looked away.

"It isn't over, Nilan. I know you love Nalana. There's a way you can be with her. Your families will come around. Don't give up."

He looked at me again and said nothing.

"It can be worked out. I know it can. You and Nalana will have a life together."

"I can't live without Nalana."

"You'll live with her. It'll take time to make it happen. You must continue talking to your parents and let them know that she's the only wife for you."

"But they won't listen. And her family won't listen. They think Allah and the ancestors don't want our marriage. That's nonsense."

"You're a strong man, Nilan. I know you'll convince them. It may take time, but you'll convince them. I know you can. I know you won't give up."

He pulled himself up and sat beside me.

"I'm hungry," I said. "I haven't eaten today. How about you? Will you eat with me?"

"If you like."

I called to Nilan's father and asked if there was food for us. He came to the door, obviously relieved. "Yes, I'll tell my wife."

"You must consider possibilities. There's always a solution. And you know I'll help any way I can."

"Will you talk to my father?"

"I will after we eat. But we both must eat. You must remain strong for your life with Nalana. And your children."

He brightened. "Yes, we want many children, both boys and girls. We have talked about it."

"And you'll have them. And they'll be good children. Like their parents."

Nilan's mother and sister entered with plates of food, placed them before us, and then left. I was hungry and attacked the food. Nilan ate tentatively and then he, too, made a big dent in the portions before us. We reminisced about some of our good times together as we ate, and before long his big smile was back in place.

"Will you talk to my father now?"

"Yes."

I went outside where Nilan's father was sitting with his wife and daughter.

"Has he eaten?" asked the father.

"Yes, we've both eaten."

"What did he say?"

"He loves Nalana very much and wants to marry her."

"That's impossible. Can't you talk some sense into him?"

"Why is it impossible?"

"The storm was a bad omen. It will be very bad if they marry."

"If not for the storm, would you let them marry?"

He was silent for a moment. "She seems like a good girl." He paused. "But our families have been enemies many years. It's not a good match."

"But Nilan loves only Nalana. Maybe it's time to stop being enemies."

"Love," he said dismissively. "That foolishness blinds young people. They don't know what marriage is best for them. They're too young to make decisions like that."

"Didn't you love your wife?"

"Of course not. She's a good wife, but we never knew this thing called love. That's why our marriage lasted. Someday Nilan will realize that we know best."

"I don't think so. If you stand in his way, you may lose your son."

"He'll grow up and realize we're right. This foolish love of young people never lasts. I've seen it many times."

I returned to the house where Nilan was still sitting in the corner.

"What did he say?"

"Probably the same thing he told you."

"They're old and foolish. They don't understand. They only know the old ways but it's not like that anymore. They won't take Nalana from me."

It was a lazy mid-morning several days later. I lay in my boat trying to think of a not-too-strenuous way to spend the day. I didn't feel like working, but my work ethic was kicking in and telling me to find Laka and see what more I could learn about her encounters with spirits. I looked up and saw a sailboat moving briskly over the waters toward me. Nilan was at its helm with two other people. They furled their sail at the edge of the moorage and paddled toward me.

"Nilan," I shouted. "Good to see you." Nalana and Basata were also in the boat.

I was more than a little curious about what was happening and waded over to meet them. "What brings you here?"

"I have a favor to ask you," said Nilan with no trace of his usual smile.

"What can I do for you?"

"Nalana and I are eloping to Sibutu. Basata is helping us."

I wasn't totally surprised. "Are you sure that's a good idea?"

"It's the only way. I pleaded with my family. I told them the storm was a freak accident and had nothing to do with me and Nalana. But they wouldn't listen. Nalana's family agreed with them. Her father never wanted our marriage and this was an excuse for him to oppose it even more. It's nonsense. Storms like that have happened before. It's the way of the world."

"I don't know," I said. "Maybe you should talk to your families some more. Wait a while. Surely something can be worked out."

"They won't listen. We've tried. They won't let me marry Nalana. If I can't marry Nalana, I'll kill myself."

"No, no," cried Nalana, speaking for the first time. "If we elope, they'll eventually accept our marriage. Not all of them are so opposed. Only the old ones. If we elope, they'll come around."

"But your families will be furious."

"They'll get over it," said Nilan. "We'll go to Sibutu where my cousin lives. Then we'll go on to Semporna where I can work. When we come back, they'll be over their anger."

"But Sibutu's far away. Are you sure you can make it in that boat?"

"We can make it. It's a good boat and Basata is a good sailor." He was silent for several moments and then repeated, "I have a favor to ask you."

"What is it?"

"This boat belongs to my father. We've taken it without his permission. My little boat would never make it to Sibutu." He paused again. "I have a hundred pesos here." He pulled an envelope from his pocket. "I want you to give this to my father tomorrow. I don't want him to think I'm a thief. But wait until tomorrow after we're gone."

"But what will you do for money in Semporna?"

"I have a little money and I'll get a job. We can stay with my cousin."

I had considerable misgivings. "Are you sure this is the right thing to do? Isn't there somewhere here in Tawi-Tawi where you can go?"

"Our families are here and they oppose the marriage. They won't take us in. If you won't give the money to my father, I'll find someone else. Maybe Masa."

"I'll give him the money but I'm concerned about you. What if you can't find a job in Semporna?"

"My cousin is there. He'll help us."

"Wait." I went into my boat and opened the tin where I kept my cash. I returned to Nilan. "Here's two hundred pesos. Take it. You'll need it in Semporna."

He looked at the money and said, "I cannot take it."

"Of course, you can. I owe you much more than this. I could never have done my research without you. Take it."

He looked at the money again and then looked at me. "I'll take it. But it's a loan. I'll pay you back. I promise."

"It's yours." I handed him the money.

"Allah will bless you," said Nalana.

"And I hope Allah watches over you," I said. "Will you send me a letter when you reach Sibutu?"

"When we reach Semporna. We don't want anyone knowing we're in Sibutu. Don't tell anyone. They'll come after us. Tell them we didn't say where we were going."

"I wish there was a better way."

"So do we, but there isn't. We must go now. I pray to Allah that we'll meet again. You are like my brother." His eyes moistened. So did mine.

They paddled the boat to the channel, hoisted the sail, and headed toward distant Sibutu barely visible on the western horizon.

The next day, about noon, I arrived at Nilan's village. I wasn't looking forward to the visit. When I approached the house, Nilan's father was standing on the deck. His wife and daughter were washing clothes. They acknowledged me but said nothing.

"I've come about Nilan," I said.

"Yes," said the father. "Come up."

I climbed the short ladder to the deck. He looked at me expectantly.

"I saw Nilan yesterday and he asked me to give you this." I handed him the envelope. The mother and sister cried quietly.

"He went to Sibutu, didn't he?"

I paused and then said, "Yes." I couldn't lie.

"Nalana and Basata were with him?"

"Yes, they were."

He opened the envelope and read the note inside, looked at the money and said, "Thank you."

He had nothing more to say. Nor did I.

I was the last person to see Nilan and Nalana. They never arrived at Sibutu and no one ever discovered what happened to them. Perhaps their boat capsized or perhaps a swift current carried them to the open sea. Or maybe they made it to Semporna where they assumed new identities and never looked back. I'd like to believe the latter, but I know it's unlikely.

I wish I could say that after their disappearance, the families realized the folly of their feud, made up and lived happily ever after. That didn't happen. Each family blamed the other. A few months after their disappearance, a cousin of Nilan was found shot in the forest behind his village and several weeks later, Nalana's brother was stabbed on his way home from school.

I have a recurring dream. I'm working late at night in the little schoolhouse at the Sanga-Sanga moorage. I look up and see Nilan at the door. He smiles his big smile and says, "I told you I'd be back and here I am." Then he disappears. I always wake up with a sad hurt in my stomach.

Fathers

Breakfast was over. I was sitting in the dining room at the Bayot Hotel watching the wet world outside and wondering if the rain would ever stop. Somewhere out there was a spectacular view of Basilan Island and the always colorful Zamboanga port, but I couldn't see it. All I could see was rain. I was in Zamboanga for an anthropology conference and some R and R. The weather was perfect during the conference, but when it ended the rain began. And it didn't stop.

If you've never experienced a tropical downpour, you don't know rain. It's like someone turned on a huge faucet in the sky and forgot to turn it off. Waterfalls cascade from roofs, streets become rivers, fields are lakes, sea is indistinguishable from land, umbrellas and raingear are useless, and eventually everything—pillows, rugs, drapes, clothing and furniture—becomes soggy from the wetness that permeates the world. My shirt was damp, my hair was damp, my beard was damp, my tablecloth was damp, my napkin was damp, my sugar was a damp lump in its clammy bowl, and my damp salt refused to exit its sodden shaker. Tired ceiling fans struggled to move the heavy, moist air in the room. I could almost hear them sloshing above me.

The waiter was refilling my coffee cup when a Caucasian man entered the dining room and sat at the table beside me. He said "Good morning" and commented on the rain in a voice suggesting New England. I returned his greeting. He studied his menu while I studied the dripping world outside, reconsidering my plans for the day. A priest named Father Donahue was originally scheduled to join me in about an hour to visit some of the sights of Zamboanga. I'd been in and out of the colorful city many times, but had never taken time to explore it. I knew the airport, the wharf, the Bayot Hotel, and the roads connecting them, but that was about it. I met Donahue several weeks earlier when he visited Father Raquet in Bongao. We discovered we'd be in Zamboanga at the same time and decided to tour the city together, but the rain put a literal damper on that plan. He called earlier and we both decided to leave on the *Jolo J* that afternoon. He would disembark at Jolo, his home base, and I would continue on to Bongao.

"Do you live in Zamboanga?" The question came from the man at the table beside me.

"No, I'm here for a conference. How about you?"

"I'm vacationing from Manila. I planned to visit the Sulu Islands, but my timing isn't too good. How long do you think this rain will last?"

His warm smile added character to his unremarkable face. He was probably in his late twenties with closely cropped dark hair and a deep tan that accentuated his lively green eyes. He was slim and of medium height.

"It's difficult to say," I said. "I remember one that lasted five days. I thought the islands were going to wash away."

"I'm told there are no flights to Jolo or Bongao."

"The rain grounded them. Even in good weather, the flights are iffy. Hopefully they'll start up again before too long, but right now the only way to reach Bongao is by slow ship. It stops at Jolo and Siasi. Do you plan to go to Bongao?"

"That was my plan. Have you been there?"

"I'm doing anthropological research down there. I'm taking the *Jolo J* back this evening. I'd hang around longer if I thought this rain would stop but that might not happen anytime soon."

He dug into his bacon and eggs and after several bites and swallows said, "I might join you. Waiting for the rain to stop seems a waste of time. At least I'll see some sights if I get on the ship."

"If the rain continues like this, you won't be seeing much but rain. But if you've never traveled on one of the inter-island cargo ships, it's an adventure. Don't expect the *Queen Mary* though."

He laughed. "I've traveled on local ships. I think I'm prepared. By the way, my name's Ron Bateson."

I told him my name and asked, "What brings you to the Philippines?"

"A Fulbright research grant. I'm an educational psychologist studying the elementary school system in Manila."

We talked about our research and then I excused myself to write some letters I wanted to post before leaving Zamboanga. We agreed to meet later and go to the ship together. I wrote the letters and worked on a research report until my hand was tired from writing and my head wrung dry of thoughts. I decided to take a break. The rain was still pounding when I returned to the dining room. The roof was suffering from the onslaught and two waiters were strategically placing pans around the room to catch water from the leaking ceiling. An elderly white couple sat solemnly at a table near the entrance sourly scanning their menus. Both were thin as rails. I smiled at them and the woman returned a small smile. The man grimaced. The only other person in the room was Ron, still sitting at the table where I left him. A bottle of San Miguel beer and two empties kept him company.

I settled into a chair beside him and a waiter materialized for my order. I ordered a beer.

Ron asked, "What time should we leave for the ship?"

I checked my watch. "In about an hour. Departure time is six, which means we probably won't leave 'til eight or later. But we should get there early so we can find good cots. And also we should pick up some food on the way. There's none onboard."

"Okay. I'll go pack. I'll meet you in the lobby in an hour."

I was packed and ready to leave so I stayed in the dining room watching the pans on the floor fill with rain and the geckoes on the ceiling chase insects. When I returned to my room, the old white couple sat at the same table, staring at plates of unappetizing food they periodically forked into their mouths. They'd not spoken since I entered the dining room, apparently having exhausted conversation years ago. I smiled when I passed them. The old man glared back.

I met Ron in the lobby. After paying our bills, we went to the portico where a bellhop waited with a *calesa*, the horse-drawn carriages still popular in Zamboanga in those days. We climbed into the *calesa*, which was only slightly less wet than outside, and the driver trotted his little horse through the puddles to the marketplace where we bought some food. At the *Jolo J*, we followed a stevedore up the gangplank, skirted stacks of cargo, and climbed a narrow staircase to an upper deck filled with army cots. We found two far enough from the rail to escape the rain and reserved a third one for Father Donahue.

A few minutes later, a rumbling laugh below and some loud, well-chosen words about the rain announced that Donahue had arrived. A tall, overweight man with Ireland written all over his round red face bounded from the staircase onto the deck sporting a broad smile of yellowish teeth. He wore the white cassock of his order, its hem wet and mud-splattered. He spotted me, waved, and moved in our direction, squeezing his way through people and cargo.

"You saved me a cot," he boomed.

"A deluxe one," I said. I introduced him to Ron. He stuffed his bag under his cot and sat down. The cot groaned.

"I've never seen rain like this," said Ron. "It's a little scary."

"I know what you mean," said Donahue. "When I experienced my first one, I thought the Biblical flood was being replayed. I'd been in Mindanao only a few months. I really timed my arrival right—the worst floods of the century and the Japanese invasion!" He pulled a flask from beneath his cassock, took a long swig, and offered it to us. "Something to warm you up?"

We declined.

"I didn't know you were here during the war," I said. "Were you with Father Raquet?"

"Indeed I was." He returned the flask to his cassock and settled onto his cot. "He and I were the first of the order to arrive in the Philippines in 1941. The Jesuits were handling these southern provinces and decided they needed help, so they asked us to send in some priests. While they were trying to figure out what to do with us, they sent us to a parish near Cotabato. We were there when the rains hit. Cases of cholera began showing up and we'd exhausted medical supplies at the clinic."

"So you're a medic too," I said.

"Sort of. Raquet and I both had a little medical background that came in handy once we got here. Two women were critically ill and needed more help than we could give them. Our drivers wouldn't take them to Cotabato because rumors were flying about the Japanese invasion. We told them the Japanese wouldn't invade in rains like this, but they wouldn't buy it. Finally, Raquet said the women had to get to the hospital and if no one else would take them, he would. I couldn't let him go alone, so I went with him. We left in pouring rain in an old panel truck. Everyone thought we were crazy— including me."

He paused and laughed. "I just arrived and already I'm boring you with my war stories. Leave it to the Irish to talk all the time. My dad always said I didn't know when to keep my mouth shut."

"You're not boring us," said Ron. "Did you make it to the hospital?"

Donahue needed no further encouragement. "When we reached the lowlands the fields were flooded, only the roadway was above water. I'll never forget that sight. We turned on to the main road and as far as the headlights could see, it was covered with rats escaping the flooded fields. There were probably other critters on the road too, but all I remember is hordes of rats. We drove slowly, but we were obviously running over them. It was awful. We entered a clump of trees and when we turned, we ran smack into the invading Japanese convoy."

"In all that rain?"

"It takes more than rain to stop the Japanese empire. We stopped and two soldiers approached and pounded on our window. Raquet told them we were trying to get to Cotabato with our patients who needed urgent medical attention. They responded in angry Japanese. Raquet tried again in English. One of them went back to the convoy and returned with an officer. He spoke English and told us we were prisoners of the Japanese empire. Raquet repeated that we had to get to Cotabato and promised we'd surrender when we returned. We were told again we were prisoners of Japan. Raquet was exasperated. He started the truck and began passing the convoy. I fully expected them to open fire on us, but for some reason they didn't. Raquet's a tough little nut. I can truthfully say that I wouldn't have had the courage to stand up to the Japanese like he did. I'm still not sure why they let us go. Maybe they had more important matters on their plate or maybe they weren't sure what to do with enemy aliens yet. Whatever the case, we made it to Cotabato with the women. We dropped them off at the hospital, picked up supplies, and headed back home. We met the convoy again and told them we were ready to surrender. An officer ordered us to our convento and told us to remain there. A couple days later they arrested us, and two weeks later we were in Manila at Santa Tomas prison." He paused, looking quietly into the night. He pulled out his flask and took another long drink from it. "So many years and so many people ago. We go through a lot of them in a lifetime."

"What a story," said Ron. We fell silent. I opened a ragged Agatha Christie novel and slipped into a gloomy English country manor where an unpopular lord met a poisonous demise. Ron wrote a letter. Donahue rolled over on his back to nap, his stomach mountainous among the slender Filipinos.

I figured out who–did–it and still wasn't sleepy so I decided to explore the deck. I stepped my way around cots to the starboard side of the ship where I was surprised to discover the old white couple from the hotel standing at the rail, gazing silently into the wet darkness.

I approached them and said, "We meet again. I didn't know we were fellow passengers."

They turned to me, startled.

"Are you going to Jolo?" I asked.

"We don't speak to strangers," hissed the old man, glaring at me as if I'd offered an indecent proposal. He turned and with his wife meekly following walked briskly away and entered one of the cabins reserved for passengers who paid extra pesos for privacy.

I shrugged, puzzled. I wandered the deck awhile and decided to return to my cot. Donahue was still sleeping and Ron was reading.

About midnight, the ship blasted its horn twice and slowly reversed from the wharf, turned, and began its southwestward trek

down the Sulu Archipelago. I stretched out on my cot, ready
for some serious sleep.

I was startled awake by the ship's horn. I bolted upright and
discovered we'd arrived at Jolo. Donahue and Ron were sitting
on their cots, watching me wake up. "What time is it?" I asked.

"A little after five," replied Donahue. "Will you two join me
at the convento for breakfast? The ship'll be here several hours."

"Sounds good to me," said Ron. I agreed.

We retrieved our bags, fell in line with the departing
passengers and faced the still-falling rain. Pedicabs waited for
passengers on the wharf. Donahue filled one and Ron and I
shared another. Minutes later we arrived at the convento, and
shortly after that we were sitting at the dining table, sipping
mugs of strong black coffee after devouring a hearty breakfast.
Donahue laced his coffee with whatever was in his flask. Again,
Ron and I declined his invitation to partake.

Nothing adorned the cement walls and tiled floor of
the dining room, but any lack of cheer in the decor was
compensated by the big breakfast and the stories of Donahue.
He was reminiscing about his early years in Jolo when the local
Muslims were none too happy about the arrival of Catholic
priests. During a pause in his stories, Ron asked him about his
time at the Santa Tomas prison during the war.

"If you have a few weeks, I'll tell you all about it," he replied jokingly, primed for another story. "It wasn't so bad initially, but it went downhill rapidly. Some of the Japanese had a cruel streak, but many of them were pretty decent. The hunger was the worse part. At first Filipinos brought us food from outside, but as the war progressed, food was in short supply for everyone. I was probably over two hundred pounds when I went in. When we were liberated, I was a hundred-and-twenty. Father Raquet fared worse. He's a little guy. When we went in he was probably about one hundred thirty, but when we came out he was only eighty pounds. He was literally skin and bones. He adores children and was so concerned about their meager rations that most of his food went to them. I don't know how he survived. We all cut back so the kids could eat, but Father Raquet gave most of his rations to them. He always said the children were our hope that places like Santa Tomas wouldn't happen again. We tried to create a community with school, lectures, concerts, sports—anything to keep our minds off our hunger and incarceration. Father Raquet was involved in it all. If it weren't for him, a lot of people would never have survived."

He became quiet and his eyes glistened.

"I'm sure you impacted many lives too," I said.

"Maybe, but nothing like Father Raquet. That man's in a class of his own. He's a saint. He's what priests are supposed to be. Some people are born good and some are born bad.

Most of us are somewhere in between. Father Raquet was born good—very, very good." He emptied his flask into his coffee mug.

After more coffee Ron and I decided to take a rainy tour of Jolo. We bought two cheap Japanese umbrellas and strolled around town but it didn't take long to decide it was no day for sightseeing. We returned to the ship where we read, napped, and ate until about midnight when the ship departed.

I leaned on the rail watching Jolo Island recede into the rain. Finally, all I could see was Tumantangis, "the mountain of tears," so-called because it's the last view departing residents see of their beloved island and the first seen by homesick returnees. I lacked emotional ties to the island and watched the mountain disappear with dry eyes.

We arrived in Siasi at about four a.m. The moon was a hazy orb struggling for visibility through the still falling rain. I stood at the rail with other insomniacs watching a crewman toss heavy mooring ropes to a stevedore on the wharf. The gangplank was rolled out once again and a groan from the ship's horn announced our arrival. Across the wharf, hoping to attract arriving passengers and crew, a few sleepy vendors offered their meager wares of cigarettes, cakes, and fruits under the awnings of closed shops. Several curiosity seekers came to meet the ship but most of the little town was still sleeping.

"Excuse me."

I turned and was surprised to see the old woman from the Bayot Hotel at my side.

"Good morning," I said.

She smiled weakly. "I want to apologize for my husband's behavior. I'm afraid he was very rude to you. He's not himself these days."

"I'm sorry to hear that."

"Old age has taken a terrible toll on him. He's become very angry and paranoid. You probably cannot believe it, but he was once a very handsome gracious man." She paused. "We sometimes become many different people as we go through life."

"You owe me no apology. I'm sorry about your husband." I looked down and noticed she was carrying a small suitcase. "Are you leaving the ship here?"

"Yes. This is the end of this stage of our journey. We're visiting our son's grave."

"He's buried here on Siasi?"

"Yes. He died here years ago—in 1940. We always wanted to visit his grave, but so many things interfered—the war, our other children. My husband has become obsessed in his old age about seeing the grave. He was our only son and my husband was very devoted to him. He talks of nothing else. It's been a long journey."

"How did your son happen to die here?"

"He was an adventurous young man traveling around the world. We're not entirely sure how he died. We were told it was cholera. This island was even more isolated back in those days so his body could not be shipped home."

"Do you have a place to stay?"

"There's a small Chinese hotel. We'll stay there. We'll go back to Zamboanga when the ship returns from Sitangkai."

I asked if there was anything I could do to help.

She replied, "No. Thank you. I wanted to let you know I appreciate your overtures of friendship. And my husband would too if he were his younger self. It's so painful to see what old age has done to him." She sighed quietly. "I must go now. Goodbye."

I watched her enter the cabin. Minutes later she appeared with her husband and they walked down the gangplank sharing a large black umbrella and carrying small suitcases. They stepped over and around puddles as they made their way up the empty street and disappeared into the rain.

It was late afternoon and we were at sea again, the rain still falling furiously. Ron was gazing into the wetness at a distant island. "Living on a little island like that must really limit your worldview," he mused.

"I suppose, but you'd be surprised how interconnected these islands are. They're not as remote as you might think. Maybe a few people have never been off that island, but most of them have."

"Nonetheless, it must be pretty exciting when someone from the outside world stops by."

"Probably so," I agreed. "Several months ago I was traveling on a launch in eastern Tawi-Tawi and we stopped at a little island. Most of the people had never seen an American. I was treated like a dignitary. They insisted on serving me a huge dinner because the American troops drove the Japanese from the islands. Which isn't entirely true. By the time Americans arrived here, Filipino guerrillas had pretty much taken care of the Japanese."

"You're lucky they liked Americans. It might've been different if you were Japanese."

"True. Or a priest."

"They're not too popular here?"

"Most are now, but they weren't always. Father Raquet had a tense reception on Simati Island when he went there to establish a school."

"What happened?"

"Simati's a fairly big island and its public school was defunct. Raquet decided it would be a good place to build a school since the youth—not to mention the adults— were almost all illiterate. The Bishop gave him the green light so he took a launch to Simati to meet with community leaders."

A sudden blast of wind showered us with rain.

"Let's go back to our cots," suggested Ron. We squeezed through the scattered cots to our own. "And what kind of welcome did he receive?"

"Rather cool. The headman and several imams met him at the wharf. They were polite but reserved and asked why he was visiting them. He explained his concern that the children were receiving no education. He told them they would be left behind the other children in Tawi-Tawi who were attending school. He emphasized that he wasn't interested in converting them to Christianity, but simply wanted to educate them. They listened politely as he proposed building a school if the community would pitch in and help. The adults could observe the classes and see that the children weren't being taught Christianity. When he finished, he asked if they had questions. They had none and told him to wait while they discussed the matter in the mosque. They left, but soon returned and politely told him they were not interested in a school and preferred teaching their children their own way. They said he could stay overnight, but in the morning they expected him to take a launch back to Bongao."

"That must have been disappointing for him."

"Maybe, maybe not. I doubt if he expected them to welcome his proposal with open arms. They served him dinner, arranged comfortable sleeping quarters, and told him they would escort him to the launch in the morning."

"And is that what happened?"

"Not quite. After he went to bed, the headman came into his room and asked if he had any medicines. His grandson had fallen and impaled his jaw on a pointed bamboo. Father always carried medicines when he traveled, knowing that treating ailments was a great entry into communities. He cleaned and bandaged the boy's wound. Word soon spread that he had medicines and before long, several people arrived with ailments. Finally, everyone left and he went to bed."

"Where did he learn medicine?"

"I'm not sure. Maybe at the seminary. Most of what he handed out was pretty basic stuff, but it worked wonders on some of the ailments."

"Did they put him on the launch the next morning?"

"The launch didn't come, but the patients kept coming. He treated them the best he could, but eventually ran out of medicine. A launch arrived in late afternoon, so he went to his room and packed his belongings. Outside, he was met by the same men who rejected his school proposal. They expressed gratitude for his kindness and said that even though he was not a Muslim, he was a man of Allah. They wanted to know more about the school he proposed to build."

"And did they build it?"

"Eventually they did. Father sent over two teachers, young Muslim men. Parents were encouraged to visit the classes and see that their children were not proselytized. Only a few students attended at first, but before long, most children were attending. And not a single person has been converted to Christianity. Nor is that likely to happen so long as Father Raquet is in charge."

"What do his superiors think of him? Isn't he supposed to be adding converts to the Catholic flock?"

"His order was founded to help the poor and disadvantaged through education and medicine. He believes he's serving his God by helping people—all people, not just Catholics. He's a rare edition. I have the greatest respect for that man and his personal religion."

When I awakened, I sensed something was different. Then I realized what it was. It wasn't raining and the world was drenched in sunshine. I joined Ron at the ship's rail.

"There really is a sun," I said.

"I was beginning to doubt it. That sun feels so damn good. What a gorgeous day."

The sea was royal blue. Above, a pale blue sky was filled with puffed-out clouds. Bongao's mountain loomed starboard and in the distance, the green slopes of Tawi-Tawi Island interrupted the brilliant aquas of the reefs. Other passengers joined us watching the islands glide by and absorbing the warm rays of the welcomed sun.

"I think Captain Jack's going to take the ship through the Sanga-Sanga channel," I said.

"Doesn't he normally?"

"No. The channel can only be navigated at high tide. Most captains never attempt it and go around the island to reach the wharf. Going through the channel cuts a good half-hour off the trip."

Captain Jack sounded the ship's horn three times and cranked up the volume on the scratchy recording of Sousa marches he usually played when he arrived in port. Villagers on either shore watched, some waving as the noisy, oversized ship slid through the narrow passage. The horn blasted repeatedly announcing our arrival and celebrating the return of sunshine. We slipped through the channel with waving villagers on either side and loudly entered Bongao's wide bay chugging our way toward the wharf and its bright red warehouse. We eased to the wharf with the Souza marches blaring our arrival at full volume.

The entire town heard us approaching and most of it congregated at the wharf to meet us. Crewmen tossed mooring ropes to waiting stevedores. A swarm of half-naked boys scrambled onto the lower deck in hopes of earning a few centavos by carrying someone's luggage. The gangplank was lowered and the first eager passengers debarked into the waiting throng at the wharf.

"So this is Bongao," said Ron, surveying the crowd.

"This is it. The metropolis of Tawi-Tawi."

"How many people live here?"

"The official census says about five thousand, but my guess is half that."

"It looks like they all came to meet the ship."

"Here comes Father Raquet." I pointed to a small man in a white cassock moving rapidly through the crowd. I waved vigorously and after several moments, he recognized me and waved back.

We retrieved our bags, walked the shaky gangplank, and pressed through the crowd to Father Raquet. He clapped me on the back and said, "I was beginning to think you decided to stay in Zamboanga—or were swallowed up by the rain." I introduced him to Ron.

"I'm hoping Captain Jack has a letter for me. I'll meet you at Santiago's after I see if he has it."

We walked to Santiago's refreshment parlor, found a table, and ordered coffee. Minutes later, Father Raquet arrived with a handful of letters. "Do you mind if I read this letter?" he asked. "I'm anxious to know what the bishop has to say."

While he read his letter, Ron and I tried to improve the coffee with sugar and canned milk, both sitting in saucers of water to discourage ants. It didn't work.

"Oh, thank God, thank God, thank God!" beamed Father.

"I take it that means good news," I said.

"Wonderful news for the people of Tawi-Tawi. The sisters are going to open a clinic in Bongao. I've been trying to get them down here for years. Finally, we'll have a full-time doctor and I won't have to watch people die who could be saved with simple medical intervention."

"I'm happy for you," I said.

"Thank you," he said. "But be happy for the people of Tawi-Tawi." He turned to Ron. "I'm sorry. I've been very self-absorbed. How long will you stay in Bongao?"

"Only overnight. I'll catch the ship when it returns from Sitangkai tomorrow. I've got to get back to Manila."

"A short visit. But the rain has stopped and you can see our beautiful islands. Please stay with me at the convento. It's not the Ritz, but it's comfortable."

"That's very kind of you."

"And plan on dinner with me. I'll ask Tia to cook up something special." He laughed. "But she'll cook whatever she wants no matter what I tell her. Sometimes it's palatable. Keep your fingers crossed for tonight. But I must run. I have a teachers' meeting. I'll see you at dinner, if not before." He drained his coffee cup and left clutching his mail with a wide smile.

"He's been trying to entice the nuns down here for years."

"What kind of nuns are they?"

"I don't remember the name of their order, but they establish clinics and hospitals in places around the world with no medical facilities. They'll be a great boon to Tawi-Tawi."

"He's a remarkable man," said Ron.

We ordered big breakfasts and wolfed them down while watching stevedores unload the ship. After filling our bellies, we made our way down Bongao's very muddy street to the convento where we left our bags. I suggested a walk around the island so Ron could take in some local color as we stretched our legs after the confining days aboard ship. He was agreeable.

When we returned to the convento, Father Raquet was sitting on the lanai watching the sun inch toward the distant horizon. "Did you walk around the island?" he asked.

"Yes. It's a lovely island," said Ron. "How did the teachers' meeting go?"

"Routine stuff. Nothing special. The shocker came later."

"What happened?"

"The head teacher from Simati arrived and told me there was a fire at the school last night. It was probably arson."

"Do you know who did it?"

"I suspect it was the disgruntled group that never wanted the school, at least not on the terms that built it. It goes back to an old family feud in the village. One side resented the other being more involved in the school and getting credit for it."

"I'm sorry," I said. "I know how much work you put into that school."

"My work's not important. What matters is that the children now have no school. I should've been more sensitive to the feud between those two groups. I'll go over tomorrow and try to reconcile the factions and get the repairs started." He smiled at us. "I'll figure it out. But enough of my problems. Are you ready to face whatever Tia's cooked for us? I told her we would eat at seven, but she insisted on dinner at six as usual." He laughed. "I don't know why I let that woman browbeat me the way she does."

Tia had indeed cooked dinner at six. When we ate at seven, it was cold soup, cold rice, cold fish, and soggy vegetables. But we were hungry and devoured the food as if it were hot from the stove of a gourmet chef. We lingered at the table over dessert and watched a moon emerge from the sea until we all agreed it was time for sleep. I fell into a bed in the room I shared with Ron and drifted to sleep without the sound of rain.

When I awakened, warm sunshine streamed through the open window. Ron was propped on pillows in his bed reading. I crawled out of bed and stepped into my jeans. "What time is it?"

"A little after seven," said Ron.

"That means breakfast is cold. Tia fries the eggs at six and puts them in the refrigerator if no one's there to eat them."

"Refrigerated fried eggs? That's a new one for me."

"They're not bad—especially in the heat of the tropics," I said, pulling on a T-shirt. We went downstairs where Father Raquet was reading a *Newsweek* magazine with a cup of coffee.

"Good morning," he said. "Are you ready for breakfast? I hope you slept well."

"We slept like rocks. After two nights on that ship with a hundred other people, your accommodations are luxurious."

"I'm leaving for Simati in about an hour to see if I can salvage the school and reconcile the battling factions." He looked at Ron and said, "I'm afraid I haven't been a very good host."

"You've been a wonderful host."

"I'm taking Ron over to the Sama Dilaut moorage. When we get back it'll probably be time for him to board the *Jolo J* for the return trip to Zamboanga."

"Hopefully I'll see more than rain this time."

"I think you will," said Father. "After a heavy rain we often have a dry spell. Let's go to the table. Tia's bringing breakfast."

A very short, dour-faced, barefooted Filipina of indeterminate old age was slapping plates on the table. She left the room and returned with a plate of very cold scrambled eggs. She left again and returned with bread, cold fried fish, and papaya.

"This is it," smiled Father Raquet. "Breakfast Tia-style."

"I'm ravenous," said Ron.

"Good thing," laughed Father. "Tia's cooking is best confronted when you're ravenous!"

"How long has she been with you?"

"Eons. Years ago her son and his wife and their two children drowned in a terrible accident near Sangasiapu. She was left with no family and no money, so I hired her to cook for me. She has a mind of her own and her own way of doing things, but she's fed me all these years. Despite my complaining, I'd be lost without her."

"Father Raquet! Father Raquet!" Someone was shouting from the street.

"Now what? Eat your breakfast. I'll be right back." He went outdoors and about ten minutes later returned, obviously upset.

"I'm sorry, but I must leave immediately. A PC officer was killed last night in a shoot-out with smugglers. His poor wife is distraught. And they have four small children." He went into his bedroom and returned wearing his white cassock.

Ron stepped forward. "I'll probably be gone when you return. It's been a pleasure meeting you. And thank you for your great hospitality. I'm sorry we didn't have more time together."

"And I'm sorry, too," said Father, grasping Ron's hand warmly. "You must come back when things are less hectic so we can spend more time together and you can see more of Tawi-Tawi."

"I'd like that. I hope you can smooth the ruffled feathers on Simati."

"I'll try. Meanwhile I must go." He hurried out the door.

We walked to the window and watched his small white figure hurry down the street.

"Does that man ever rest?" asked Ron.

"Not too often. He's got more stamina than ten men twice his size. Not to mention a heart that would fill this room."

When Ron and I returned from the moorage, we bought food at the marketplace for his return trip. Then we stopped at Santiago's for a late lunch and watched the final loading of the *Jolo J.*

"This has been a great trip," said Ron. "I've been planning it most of my life."

"To Bongao?"

"Not exactly Bongao." He paused. "Can you keep a secret?"

"I've been known to do so."

"I'm serious. Will you promise not to repeat what I'm going to tell you?"

"I promise," I said. "But are you sure you want to tell me?"

"Yes. I want to tell you. You've taken this journey with me."

"Okay. I'm listening."

"Father Raquet is my father."

"You mean," I paused, "your real father? Your biological father?"

"Yes."

"And he doesn't know it?"

"Right."

"Wow!" I was dumbfounded.

"I never knew who my father was. My mother always avoided questions about him when I was a kid and I soon realized she didn't want to talk about him, so I stopped asking. She married a really decent man and he adopted me and took care of my father needs. But I was always curious about my real father and had a love/hate relationship with the fantasy man I created. After my stepdad died and not long before Mom died, she told me about him."

"What changed her mind?"

"I'm not sure. Maybe she thought I had a right to know, especially when she began facing her own mortality. She and Father Raquet were high school sweethearts. He became increasingly involved in the church during his senior year and after graduation decided to enter the seminary. He was there when Mom discovered she was pregnant with me. But serving God was so important to him she decided not to tell him. She knew he would leave the seminary to be with her and she couldn't make him do that. So she never told him."

"And you decided to come to the Philippines and look him up?"

"Sort of. I applied for the Fulbright because I was genuinely interested in the research project, but equally important it would allow me to look up my father."

"What did you plan to do when you met him?"

"I always thought I'd confront him. Most of my life I resented him. But when I discovered he didn't even know about me, it put a different wrinkle on things."

"I can see that it would."

"After learning about his life here in the Philippines and meeting him, my feelings toward him have changed entirely. He's made a much greater contribution to the world as a priest than he would have as my father. I had a wonderful mother and I ended up with a great stepdad. And the people here got Father Raquet. I think we all got a good deal."

The *Jolo J* blasted its horn, announcing its departure. Ron stood and said, "Time to leave. Promise you'll look me up in Manila when you come up. I'm really glad I ran into you. One of Father Raquet's angels must have sent you." He gave me a big bear hug.

I laughed and hugged him back. "Or one of his—whatever. Enjoy your trip."

"I will." He picked up his bag and started toward the door. He turned and winked at me, "Remember, it's our secret."

"Scout's honor. Our secret."

He ran up the gangplank and waved from the deck. The *Jolo J* sounded a final farewell and eased away from the wharf. I ordered another cup of coffee and watched the ship move into the bay and slowly disappear behind an island.

The Surf at Mata Matata

lay on my back in excruciating pain listening to the escalating cacophony of the darkening forest. I couldn't move. Wild pigs, snakes, dog-sized lizards, and maybe even crocodiles lived in the forest. Each sound triggered my imagination as the darkness thickened.

I was in the remote eastern Tawi-Tawi village of Mata Matata investigating a small community of Sama Dilaut at its outskirts. After hiking halfway around the island, I realized I couldn't make it back to the other side before nightfall. I asked a fisherman at the beach if a shortcut through the interior would return me to the other side. He said it would and gave me directions. I thanked him, found the trail, and hurried down the path. About ten minutes into the forest, I stumbled over a root and fell, the small of my back hitting a rock. Pain shot though my body like a million electrical currents and I couldn't move. I initially hurt too much to be scared, but as the pain turned to numbness, I realized the seriousness of my predicament. The chances of someone discovering me were slim since the locals avoided the forest at night, believing it was inhabited by spirits of various stripes. Insects hummed like a discordant orchestra, occasionally interrupted by an animal sound. Beyond the forest, I heard the muffled pounding of the surf.

I tried to move, but I couldn't. I felt nothing. If a crocodile bit off my arm, I wouldn't feel anything. As I was thinking this might be the end of a budding career in anthropology, I heard voices approaching.

"Help!" I shouted as loud as I could, which wasn't very loud.

The voices didn't hear me and continued talking.

"Help!" I shouted again, this time in Sinama.

They suddenly stopped.

"I've fallen," I said. "Please help me."

"Who are you?" asked a suspicious voice.

"An American," I said. I hoped they liked Americans.

A flashlight was switched on and its beam swept the path until it found me. Two men and a boy approached.

"Are you the American who lives with the boat people?" the older of the two men asked.

"Yes. I was walking to the other side of the island when I fell and hurt my back. I can't move. Can you help me?"

They came nearer and squatted beside me.

"What can we do?" asked the older man.

"Is there a house nearby where you can take me?"

He was silent for a moment. "The only nearby house is Mr. Garcia's."

"I can't walk. I'll have to be carried. I'll make it worth your while if you help me."

"Don't worry about that. We'll help you." He spoke to the other man. "You and Timba go to the Garcia house and see if someone can help us move this American. Mr. Garcia's a good man. He'll help us. I'll stay here until you return. Take the light." He handed them the flashlight and they walked away hurriedly leaving us in darkness.

"You're a very kind man," I said, "and I'm very grateful to you."

"We're all Allah's children. We must look after one another."

"May Allah always bless you," I said, repeating a common phrase of the local Muslims.

We talked as we awaited the others' return. I told him about my excursion around the island and my decision to take the shortcut through the forest.

"You're lucky that we, too, were delayed," he said. "We were visiting my sister and left late. No one uses this trail at night."

"Are there dangerous animals in the forest?"

"Nothing dangerous. Some harmless snakes and lizards. And, of course, birds."

"No crocodiles or wild pigs?" I asked.

"No, not on this island." He smiled at my naiveté and turned toward the voices we heard approaching. We saw the beams of two flashlights.

"Papa," called the boy. "We've come with help."

They joined us accompanied by two young men, both dressed in white shorts and T-shirts. I immediately recognized them as northern Filipinos. They expressed concern over my situation.

"You have hurt your back?" said one of them in English.

"Yes. I can't move."

The second one carried a bamboo frame about six feet long, criss-crossed with rattan. It looked like a bed frame. "We'll carry you to Mr. Garcia's house."

They placed the frame beside me and inched me toward it. The pain was wrenching and I couldn't stifle a yell. The old man broke a small limb from a nearby tree. "Bite on this," he instructed, placing it between my teeth. "Let us move him quickly." The four men, two at my shoulders and two at my hips, quickly transferred me to the rig. I spit out the stick and screamed as pain shot through my body.

"You'll be alright," said the old man, holding my hands. "We'll not move you until the pain goes away." The three faces of the other men expressed grave concern, but the old man looked at me with gentle compassion. The boy was scared out of his wits.

Slowly the pain subsided. "I think I'm ready," I said.

The men slowly and quietly lifted me. The boy walked ahead illuminating the path with a flashlight. A man at my feet held the other flashlight.

They walked slowly and the transport was surprisingly smooth. They turned from the main path and took a less-traveled trail up a gentle slope that turned sharply and then dissipated into a clearing where a brightly lit house stood. We approached it, climbed steps to a lanai, and entered.

The room was blindingly white after the darkness of the forest. The man who greeted us wore a white T-shirt and white trousers, the bamboo furniture was upholstered in white, and the half-shell of a huge white bivalve filled with white orchids dominated one side of the room. Pastel mats were scattered over the split-bamboo floor and large pastel shells hung from the rafters of the open beamed ceiling. I was carried into a bedroom where my bearers placed me on a bed and began easing me from the rack.

"Please. Don't move me yet." I wasn't up to the pain I knew would accompany the transfer. "Maybe the pain will subside and I can move later." They stepped back. "Thank you so much," I said. "I'm grateful to all of you."

"Mr. Garcia will be in," said one of the men in white. After a few words of concern from the men who initially found me, they all left the room.

I surveyed the soft yellow room, a corner room with large windows on its outer walls. Intricately woven mats of pastel shades hung on two walls. A rattan lounge chair and a chest of drawers were the only furniture besides my bed and a night table. This was a house unlike any I'd seen in Tawi-Tawi.

"I'm sorry about your accident." A man stood in the door. "I am Gregorio Garcia. Is there anything I can do to make you more comfortable?"

He was a Filipino, but his physical type would easily blend into any number of Asian countries or even Latin America. His beauty, however, would have attracted attention wherever he went. He was one of those remarkable mixes of Filipino, Spanish and American. Women of such blends are frequently exquisitely beautiful, but sometimes the men are too beautiful. Not this man. Woman or man, gay or straight, would acknowledge his striking beauty. His age was indeterminate, but he was not young.

"You're very kind to take me in," I said, "and I greatly appreciate it."

"I'm glad I was nearby to help you. Unfortunately, we have no doctor on this island, only the local practitioners. Do you think you are injured badly?"

"I'm not sure. My back has gone out before, but the pain was never like this. Usually after a couple hours, I'm okay. Do you have any aspirin? Sometimes they work for me."

"Yes, I do. One minute." He left the room and moments later returned with a bottle of aspirin and a glass of water. He shook two tablets from the bottle and handed them to me. I tried to rise onto my elbow, but the pain in my back prevented it.

"Wait," he said. "I have straws." He left the room and returned with a straw. He placed it in the glass of water. I put the aspirin in my mouth and he raised the pillow beneath my head so I could suck water into my mouth and swallow the tablets.

"Would you prefer to be alone?"

"No. Please stay."

"You're the American living with the boat-people?"

I replied that I was and asked how he knew about me.

He laughed. "This is a small island. Everything is known. Especially when a red-bearded American arrives with the boat-people."

"I suppose," I said. I briefly told him about my research.

"You're an adventuresome man to come here alone and live with the sea gypsies."

"And you? You don't seem a native of Mata Matata."

He smiled and sat in the chair. "Does it show? No, I am not. I grew up in Manila."

"And what brought you here?"

"A long story," he said, "but I'll give you the short version. Several years ago, I decided I wanted a beautiful place far removed from Manila. I spent several weeks traveling throughout the Philippines until I found Mata Matata. As soon as I arrived here, I knew this was the place. I love the sound of the constant surf, and I love the isolation."

"It's a beautiful island. And the surf—the sound is mesmerizing."

"My friends in Manila think I'm crazy, a Christian Filipino living with Moros. They thought I'd be killed in a week. You know how they are in Manila—'The only good Moro is a dead Moro.' The Mata Matata people are among the finest people I've ever known. I've had no trouble since I arrived."

"Do you live here full-time?"

"No. I come down several times a year for a few weeks. Sometimes a couple of months. Whenever I need a break from the ugly, dirty chaos of Manila."

"You have a lovely home here."

"Yes, I do. I didn't spare expenses. I've invested wisely over the years with the help of some of my wealthy clients. I designed the house myself and oversaw its construction. I wanted it clean, light, and airy with something beautiful wherever my eyes wandered. I leased the land from the old headman of the village. He's a dear man, probably a retired pirate, but a dear man." He stood. "How thoughtless of me. You must be hungry. I'll tell the cook to prepare something for you."

"I'm not too hungry. Perhaps some soup. Or a sandwich."

"Of course. I'll be right back."

Several minutes later he returned. "Is the aspirin providing any relief?"

"Yes, I think so. The pain has diminished."

"Good. I'll leave you to your privacy. Here's the aspirin." He set a bottle on the bedside table. "And here's a bell." He placed a small silver bell beside the aspirin. "If you need anything, ring the bell and Manuel will come. If you need to use the toilet, he will help you. Is there anything else I can do for you?"

"You're very kind. I should let my Sama Dilaut friends know what happened to me. They're expecting me."

"They probably know already. The men who brought you here said they would tell them. I hope your pain subsides and you're able to sleep."

"Thanks," I said. "You've been very kind to me."

"I've received many kindnesses in my life. I try to return some of them. Good night."

He left. Minutes later Manuel arrived with a sandwich and soup. He placed the tray on the bedside table and propped me up with pillows so I could better eat. I thanked him and he left. My appetite returned when I began eating and I devoured all the food. I rang the bell and Manuel reappeared.

"You are finished, sir? Would you like more?"

"No, thank you. Could you help me ease off this carrier? It's rather uncomfortable."

"Of course," he said. "I'll get Reynaldo to help me."

He left and returned with the other young man who helped carry me to the house. I offered what little assistance I could as they eased me from the carrier to the mattress.

They spread a white sheet over me, extinguished the lamp, and left. Minutes later I was sleeping.

I awakened to brilliant sunshine and the sound of surf. One of my windows offered a view of the beach and distant white waves crashing on the reef. The other was filled with the startling brilliance of magenta bougainvillea. Cautiously, I moved to test my back. The pain was gone, but when I tried to sit it returned and I yelled involuntarily. Within moments, Manuel appeared.

"Are you alright, sir?"

"Still some pain," I said, easing back onto the mattress.

He gave me aspirin with a glass of water and I downed them.

Gregorio appeared at the door. "Good morning," he said. "Are you feeling better?" He wore only a white sarong.

"Considerably," I said. "Some of the pain is still there, but my flexibility is returning." He looked older in the morning sunlight. He was no less handsome, but his youthful beauty seemed somewhat inappropriate in his middle-aged face. He was probably forty. His chest was full and still firm, his skin smooth and flawlessly golden.

"Would you like some breakfast?" he asked. "I'm about to take mine. With your permission, I'll join you."

"Thank you. I'd like that."

"Manuel," he said. "We'll have breakfast in here." Manuel left the room. Gregorio sat in the lounge chair and said, "I hope you slept well last night."

"I woke up only once."

Manuel returned with two steaming mugs of coffee. He handed one to each of us, placed sugar and milk on the table, and departed.

"What do you do in Manila?" I asked.

"I'm a whore," he said unhesitatingly. "A very expensive whore."

I was somewhat taken aback but tried not to register it.

"Do I shock you?"

"'Shock' isn't quite the word. 'Surprise' maybe."

"I'm a very expensive call boy. Call 'man' these days. I'm not exactly a boy anymore." He laughed. "I also find companions for lonely men. What do you call a male 'madam'? I do that too. But occasionally I grow tired of it all. That's when I come to my beautiful Mata Matata and lose myself in the sound of the surf."

"Did you grow up in Manila?" I asked, sipping my coffee. It was very strong and very good. I told Gregorio so.

"Yes, I grew up in Manila. More specifically, on the streets of Manila. Obviously I had a father, but I never knew him and I have only dim memories of a mother. I assume she was my mother. I vaguely remember a woman around when I was a small child. She left me with an old man. I have no idea what my real name is, if I ever had one. I chose my name. Gregorio is the name of a movie star I liked. One of the whores who sometimes let me sleep in her room and gave me food was named Garcia. Thus I am Gregorio Garcia."

"Did you literally live on the streets?"

"Until I was about twelve or thirteen. I'm not sure of my age. I slept wherever I could and ate whatever I could find. I ran with a group of boys and we managed to survive. Some people were kind to us and we learned to exploit them. But some were very unkind and we avoided them. I learned that some men found me attractive and I began turning tricks at an early age. I lived in a whorehouse for a while. They took most of the money I turned, but they fed me and gave me a place to sleep."

"You never went to school?"

"Not until I was about twelve. Some nuns began helping street children. One befriended me and asked me to attend school so I began attending classes. I liked school and learned to read and write rather quickly." He paused. "Are you really interested in all this, or just making conversation?"

"Your story is fascinating."

Manuel arrived with breakfast. I was suddenly ravenous. "What a spread," I said.

"I hope you like it."

A brightly colored parrot landed on the window sill near my bed. "What a beautiful bird," I said. "I've never seen one like it in the islands."

"I brought it from Manila. I've brought several beautiful birds here. Many of the native birds are beautiful too. I feed them so they'll stay around the house. Their beauty gives me pleasure. I want nothing but beauty when I come to Mata Matata. I planned this house so wherever I look I see beauty. I've seen enough ugliness. I leave that in Manila. Here I want only beauty."

"Do Manuel and Reynaldo stay here when you're in Manila?"

"There's always someone here. Manuel and Reynaldo are here now. They were street kids too. I found them when they were young and sent them to school. They're in college now and will return to Manila to finish school. I pay for their education, but after graduation they're on their own."

"Did you go to college?"

"I majored in art." He laughed. "Almost as practical as philosophy. But I never planned on having a career. I learned early that I could make enough money in the sex trade to support the life I wanted. Several older men remembered me in their wills. Many old men are lonely and hungry for intimacy, especially old white men. I gave them intimacy and they gave me money. It worked for all of us."

He offered the parrot some toast which it greedily devoured. "I'm a rich man," he said matter-of-factly. "I have a knack for making money and investing it wisely."

Manuel came with more coffee and took our emptied trays away. I watched him leave.

"He's very good-looking, isn't he?" said Gregorio.

"Yes," I acknowledged.

"If you want him, I'm sure he'd be happy to accommodate you. No offence, but you're not my type. I prefer older men."

"Thanks," I said, slightly embarrassed, "but I decided early in the game that sex would complicate fieldwork."

"Probably," he said. "But don't you get horny?"

"I make occasional trips to Manila."

"Let me know the next time you go. I'll give you some contacts."

"Thanks," I said, uncomfortably.

"I'm going to the gardens," he said, standing up. "When you can walk I'll show you my gardens. I love flowers. Would you like a bath? Manuel will help you."

"I'd like that very much."

"I'll tell him. Is there anything else you need?"

"No, thanks. You've been extremely kind. I hope I can someday repay you."

"Don't be concerned. I'm sure you've extended kindnesses to people. And you will again. That's your repayment." He left the room.

I still wore the shorts and T-shirt I had when I fell in the forest and was feeling more than a little grubby. I looked out the window at the brilliant bougainvillea. Two yellow birds landed on the sill, their colors startling against the magenta. The view from the other window swept over the trees of the forest to the beach and beyond to the open sea. If the views from the other windows were like the ones in my room, Gregorio had certainly succeeded in surrounding himself with beauty.

As I mused on the spectacular colors of the tropics, Manuel arrived with a basin of hot water, soap and towels. I rose onto my elbows while he pulled my T-shirt up my torso and slipped it from my arms and over my head. When he finished bathing me, he toweled me dry and covered me with a light sheet.

"Let's prop you up so you'll be more comfortable," he suggested. I rose onto my elbows again and he arranged pillows behind me until I was comfortably propped into a reading position. He placed some reading material on the bedside table.

"Ring the bell if you need anything." He left the room.

The newspaper was a two-week old copy of the *Manila Times*, but it was fresh news to me. I hadn't seen a newspaper in months. Copies of *The New Yorker* and an Asian edition of *Newsweek* were even older. I read, catching up on events that were already history. After about an hour, I became drowsy and drifted into a nap. When I awakened, Manuel was standing in the doorway.

"Would you like some lunch?" he asked.

"Yes. Very much."

"Mr. Garcia will be unable to join you. He's having one of his bad days."

After lunch, I spent the afternoon reading and dozing. Evening brought another great meal from Manuel. I asked him about Gregorio and was told he was still under the weather. I read more after dinner and then fell into a deep sleep.

I awakened to a sun-filled room with the early morning sounds of the forest providing accompaniment to the faraway surf. I rolled over and leaned on my elbow and realized my back wasn't hurting. I eased to the edge of the bed, slowly sat up, and cautiously lowered my legs over the side. Still no pain. I debated whether to try standing. I slowly slipped off the bed onto my feet. No pain yet, only soreness and stiffness. I took a tentative step. Manuel appeared in the doorway and looked at me. I realized I was nude.

"You're walking, sir!" he exclaimed.

"Yes. Baby steps, but I'm walking."

"Congratulations!" said Gregorio, joining Manuel in the doorway and ignoring my nudity.

"And congratulations to you," I said. "Are you feeling better?"

"Much better," he said. "But more importantly, you are better. Would you care to join me for breakfast on the lanai?"

"By all means."

"Find him a sarong," Gregorio said to Manuel. "I'll meet you on the lanai." They left and Manuel returned with a white sarong which I wrapped around my waist.

With Manuel at my side, I cautiously made my way into the living room. It was sun-filled and even brighter than I remembered the night of my arrival. White and lavender orchids were scattered about the room. An open ceiling soared above me. The back windows looked into the greens of the forest while front doors opened onto a covered lanai.

I stepped onto the lanai. Gregorio greeted me from the table where he sat with a mug of coffee. "Your coffee is waiting," he said, directing me to the chair beside him.

I made it to the chair and eased into it. "Still a bit sensitive," I explained as I found a comfortable position. "What a view!"

The view was an elaboration of the one from my bedroom window. The village was scattered beneath us along a white sand beach that merged into a wide reef filled with brilliant aqua shades stretching to the incoming surf fed by the brilliant blue Sulawesi Sea beyond. A crackling cerulean sky hosted white clouds. The distant, muffled roar of the surf provided an acoustical backdrop.

"This is my favorite place," said Gregorio. "I spend hours here absorbing the view and the sound of the surf." He poured me a mug of coffee. "I'm glad you feel better."

"Thanks. And I'm glad you're better."

"For the present, I am," he said. "But let's not talk about illness on such a beautiful morning." He turned and called through the open doors, "We're ready for breakfast, Manuel."

Moments later, Manuel appeared with a tray filled with dishes that he placed before us. We made conversational noises while consuming the food and then concluded breakfast with more coffee served by the omnipresent Manuel.

"When will you return to Manila?" I asked.

"Perhaps in another week. There are matters that I must attend to. Increasingly, I find it difficult to return to Manila. I'd rather stay here absorbing this beauty. It is the closest thing to religion for me."

"Are you Catholic?"

He paused. "In a way, I suppose I am since I've lived my life in this Catholic country. But if you mean do I believe in God, Jesus, Mary, and all that, no, I'm not Catholic. And you?"

"My parents gave me the gift of no religion. They weren't atheists. There simply was no tradition of religion in their families. Maybe the Christian missionaries never made it to that part of Scotland."

"Why do you say it was a gift?"

I paused. "It left my mind open to possibilities. No preconceived religious notions through which my experiences were filtered."

"The nuns taught me plenty of religion, but none of it stuck. So much of it seemed fantastical. The miracles, the virgin birth, the resurrection. I saw nothing in my experiences that allowed me to believe or accept most of the Bible. What kind of god would allow such horrible suffering that exists in this world? What kind of god would abandon a small boy in the streets to sex-starved men? But I greatly admire the nuns' work with street children. Most of my money will go to their charity when I die."

"No argument here."

"The sky, the sea, the surf. They're my religion. They're my gods. They're where I want to go when I die. Not some place in heaven populated by people from earth. I want no more people when I die. I've seen enough people. Enough ugliness, too much. I want only beauty."

We gazed silently at the surf. A monkey jumped from a tree onto the lanai. He stared at us curiously, returned to the tree, and scampered from limb to limb into the forest.

"Don't you ever become lonely here?" I asked.

"Never. Sometimes I have too many visitors. A naval patrol boat from Batu-Batu occasionally stops by. Sometimes a priest from Tabawan visits to check on my soul. I have friends in the village. Other friends sometimes come down from Manila, but most of them are too terrified to visit Moro country. Just as well. I don't want visitors." He paused. "But don't misunderstand me. I'm enjoying your company."

"And I, yours. Have you visited the States?"

"I have. I enjoyed the trip, but unlike many Filipinos, I've no desire to live there. I love the Philippines. Not the cities. Here. Where else can you find beauty like this?" He spread his arms to the panorama before us.

The next day I felt well enough to venture away from the lanai. Gregorio showed me his beautifully landscaped grounds. One side was planted in brilliant bougainvillea, some colors I'd never seen before. A shaded corner was filled with orchids and anthuriums. Bushes of red, white, and pink hibiscus splashed color throughout. A pond at the back hosted multicolored koi swimming among white lotus. Gregorio had achieved his aim. My eyes found beauty wherever they wandered.

"Do you think you can walk to the beach?" he asked. It was late afternoon. "The sunsets are frequently spectacular."

"If we walk slowly I think I can handle it."

"Good. You can watch me swim. If I feel up to it, I swim each day."

We followed a sandy path that wandered through the village. A few curious villagers greeted us. Gregorio spoke to them in Sinama and they returned his greetings with smiles. At the beach, he led me to a cluster of rocks where we sat. About ten feet away, the sea lapped at the sand.

"This is another of my favorite places," said Gregorio.

"This island has an abundance of beautiful places."

"Yes," he said. "And I have explored them all. I probably know this island better than most local people. Someday when we are both stronger, perhaps I'll show it to you."

"I would like that."

"On the other side of the island is a site you might find interesting. I think it's either an old mosque or the ruins of a fort. I found pieces of porcelain there. Probably Chinese." He stood. "I think I'll swim."

He pulled off his white T-shirt, undid his sarong and stood nude. His body was losing some of its firmness, but he was still in great shape. Again, I was impressed by his flawless golden skin.

"I'll be back soon," he said, walking toward the water.

He waded into the sea until he was in waist-high water. He swam toward the surf with strong easy strokes, sometimes stopping to float on his back, sometimes wading in shallow water. I watched him, enjoying the late afternoon warmth of the sun, and the gentle breeze blowing from the sea. After about a half-hour, he swam toward me. He waded onto the beach, shook, and brushed the water from his thick black hair and sat beside me.

"You're a good swimmer," I said.

"Yes. I love the sea. I was born in Manila near the sea, but I didn't see it until I was about fourteen. I fell in love with it instantly and never stopped loving it. But my strength is waning and my swimming days are numbered."

"Are you ill?"

"Yes, very ill. I have cancer. Terminal cancer."

I was taken aback and didn't know what to say. Finally I said, "I'm sorry. I knew you weren't well yesterday, but I had no idea why."

"You couldn't know. I have good days and bad days. I try to make the most of the good ones and not let the bad ones get me down."

"I admire your courage."

"Courage? Is that what it is? I simply want to enjoy whatever life is left for me. I'm not sure that's courage."

We looked toward the surf where the sun was rapidly dropping to the horizon.

"Are you afraid of death?" he asked.

I thought a moment. "No, not afraid. It's simply the end. But I'd rather not suffer. I want to go quickly. But I'm not ready yet. There are still things I want to do. And some people I don't want to leave."

"I used to think that way. Of course, I would like to avoid pain. And I have enough morphine for that. But there's not much more I want to do. I've seen as much of the world as I care to see. I think I know the nature of the world, at least the nature of people. And it's not too appealing."

"I've known some good people."

"Goodness is a luxury. Strip the good people of their comforts and securities and tempt them and they turn into something else. I've sold my body to those good people. You'd be amazed and appalled at some of the ways they achieve their pleasure."

"But what about all the good people out there who haven't sought you?"

"They've found others like me. And I don't mean only sex. People are inherently selfish. After they've satisfied their selfish needs then they can be good. Goodness is a luxury." He paused and laughed. "You probably think I'm a jaded, cynical old queen."

"No. I share some of your views."

The sun dropped onto the horizon and the white surf slowly turned crimson. The sky was filled with red clouds. The sand around us became red. Gregorio was red. I was red. The world was red.

"That is God," murmured Gregorio, gazing into the sunset. "That's where I want to die. I want to swim beyond the surf and become the sea, become the beauty of a spectacular sunset. I want to die in the beauty I was never allowed in life."

Two days later I left Mata Matata on a launch for Bongao. It was raining when I arrived in Bongao so I used the weather as an excuse to delay fieldwork and stay with Father Raquet for a couple of days while my back mended.

When the rain stopped and my back was better, I jumped into a flurry of activities. It was *bulan matai*, or "dead moon" as the Sama Dilaut call the period of the month when the moon is not visible, a time when Sama Dilaut families descend on Bongao to sell their dried fish from the previous month's fishing. It was also the time when ceremonies were held at the Sanga-Sanga moorage. For about a week, I attended weddings, circumcision, and healing ceremonies. By now I knew most

Sama Dilaut families and my presence didn't disrupt the events. In fact, my camera, note-taking, and tape recorder were expected.

It was the season of the year when some Sama Dilaut families planted small gardens on Sanga-Sanga Island. I accompanied them to their gardens and watched them prepare the soil, noted the crops they planted, and documented the divisions of labor that made it all happen. It was also shark-fishing season and I spent several harrowing days at sea with Masa in pursuit of those beautiful deadly creatures.

Throughout all this activity, I occasionally thought of Gregorio and his lovely home. But Mata Matata was at the other end of Tawi-Tawi and I seldom met anyone from there. About three months after I left Gregorio, a Muslim friend who operated a launch throughout the islands told me he planned to visit eastern Tawi-Tawi. Things were slow at the moorage so I decided it was a good time to take a break and see some of the islands I'd never seen—and visit Gregorio, if he wasn't in Manila. I slept overnight on the launch and we left Bongao on a dawn high tide.

We arrived at Mata Matata at noon. I grabbed my bag, jumped onto the long pier that extended from the island and walked to Gregorio's house. When I entered the grounds, I saw him seated on the lanai wearing his white sarong.

"What a pleasant surprise!" he said, spotting me. "Only this morning I was thinking of you. Come and join me. Have you eaten?"

I climbed the steps to the lanai and he extended his hand. I took it and said, "Yes, I have. Thanks."

I tried not to register surprise, but I was shocked by his appearance. He looked twenty years older than when I last saw him. He'd lost considerable weight and his once firm golden muscles hung loosely from his frame. His face was sunken and his eyes stared from dark sockets. His black hair was streaked with gray. He'd probably stopped dyeing it.

"I'm glad you're here," I said. "I was afraid you might be in Manila."

"I've been back two weeks." He motioned me into the chair beside him. "I'm finished with Manila. I've wrapped up all my affairs there and will not return. As you can see, I'm not doing too well." He held out his thin arms.

"I'm sorry," I said, lamely.

He shrugged. "I don't have much pain. When I do, I take more morphine. I live on it these days. I've lost my strength and energy. Some days, I can hardly get out of bed, but I have some good days. You lucked out. I've been having some good ones."

"I'm glad."

"I'm nothing but a bag of bones. I've lost twenty-five pounds." He laughed. "What happened to that gorgeous man everyone wanted to sleep with? Now I'd have to pay someone to sleep with me. But on the other hand, there's probably some kinky man out there who gets his rocks off by having sex with dying men." He laughed again. "Fortunately, sex is the last thing on my mind these days."

"Is Manuel still here?"

"Oh yes. Loyal Manuel. He's gone to the market to buy fish for dinner. He'll stay with me until the end. But enough of me. What have you been up to since we last met?"

"More of the same," I said and offered a brief summary of my activities.

"I admire you. You're still curious about the world and trying to figure it out. I figured it out long ago. And once I figured it out, I lost my curiosity. Since then I've been simply navigating the daily rituals of surviving—sleeping, eating, and whatever amusements I can find. But let's talk about something else. I've been visiting some of my favorite places on the island, probably for the last time. Remember I told you about a site I thought was either the ruin of a mosque or a fort? It's about a twenty-minute walk from here. Would you like to see it?"

"I would if you're up to the walk."

"I'm not in the grave yet. I'm feeling better today than I have in some time. Manuel will join us."

Soon we were walking a sandy path that edged the beach with the surf pounding a rhythmic accompaniment to our conversation. We turned from the path and followed a narrower one into the forest to a clearing scattered with large rocks.

Several coral tombstones were clustered to one side. I expected more.

"What makes you think it's a mosque or fort? It looks like a pile of rocks and an old cemetery."

"Some local people say it was once a fort, others say it was a mosque. Look at the stones carefully. They've been cut and shaped. There's a low wall near the graves made of coral stone cut to fit tightly together."

We examined the coral stones. He was correct. They had been shaped. I hadn't seen such construction elsewhere in the islands.

"These are very old tombstones," said Gregorio. "See how elaborately they're carved? Some have animal and human motifs. These are probably pre-Islamic. Islam doesn't allow such ornamentation. One of the mosques in the village has a foundation made of cut stones like this. I think it's probably the first mosque built here—maybe built on the foundation of a pre-Islamic structure."

"You should be an anthropologist." I was impressed by his interpretation.

He laughed. "Maybe in another life. This one's almost used up."

We retraced our steps. By the time we reached the house, the sun was setting.

I slept late the next morning. I heard the dawn call to prayer from the village and drifted back to sleep. When I awakened again, I went to the lanai where Gregorio was sitting with a cup of coffee. He smiled as I sat beside him.

Manuel appeared with my coffee and left to inform the cook we were ready for breakfast.

"How are you feeling?" I asked.

"I feel good. I was tired last night, but slept it away. I'm ready to take on the world. Do you have plans for the day?"

"I think I'll walk to the other side of the island and check out the Sama Dilaut moorage there. It's a seasonal moorage and I'm curious to see how many houseboats are there and what they're up to."

"Always the anthropologist," laughed Gregorio. "You're supposed to be on vacation."

"It's mostly vacation. I've never seen the eastern side of the island, so it'll be mostly sightseeing. Are you up to joining me?"

"I think I'll pass. I want to conserve my energy for a swim this afternoon. I haven't swum in several days. Would you like Manuel to accompany you?"

"Thanks, but I think I can find my way. And I promise no shortcut where I might end up on my back again."

After breakfast, I walked through the village and continued along the sandy path at the beach. A few people along the way smiled greetings, but for the most part I was alone. It was early afternoon when I arrived at the village. The villagers' Sinama was different from the dialect I knew, but similar enough to allow conversation. An old man invited me to his house, but I explained my time was limited and I wanted to visit the Sama Dilaut houseboats moored on the reef at the other end of the village. He accompanied me with several curious children.

I waded out to the boats and recognized two families. I wandered the moorage, talking to individuals and discovering kin ties to people I knew in the western moorages. It was mid-afternoon when I began my return trip. Beyond the village, I found a shade tree, sat beneath it, and recorded my observations in my journal. The sun was far in the west when I climbed the steps to Gregorio's house.

Manuel appeared and I asked him, "Is Gregorio resting?"

"No. He's gone for a swim. He's having one of his good days. Would you like a drink?"

"Maybe some water. Then I think I'll join Gregorio at the beach."

Manuel left and returned momentarily with a glass of cold water. I sipped it, watching the sun inch toward the horizon. The cloud formation promised a spectacular sunset.

I left the lanai and walked through the village to the beach where the sun was sending red and gold explosions into the sky and over the surface of the sea. I stopped at the rocks where Gregorio and I previously sat. Folded neatly atop one of them were his white sarong and T-shirt. I turned toward the sunset and looked for him, but the brilliant rays precluded everything but color. I sat beside the rocks and watched the surf burst in like molten lava. As the sun eased into the sea, grays and blues replaced the reds and golds, and then suddenly the world was dark.

I sat in the warm darkness, thinking of Gregorio and waiting for him to emerge from the sea. But as the darkness deepened into blackness, my suspicion that he would not return grew. Still I waited, watching the white breakers roll onto the beach. Finally I stood, picked up Gregorio's shirt and sarong, and walked toward the village. A full moon emerged above the forest, drenching the dark world in muted light as the surf of Mata Matata sounded on the distant reef.

The Ista Bilu

I t was one of those times when planes weren't flying to Tawi-Tawi. I was trying to reach Manila to meet a friend coming in from Tokyo and was more than a little frustrated when the plane didn't arrive on the third scheduled day.

Tawi-Tawi had only sporadic telecommunication with the outside world and the Philippine Air Lines office in Bongao never knew whether a plane was coming until it appeared in the sky. It was scheduled to arrive on Tuesday and Saturday, so on those days I took a launch from Bongao to Sanga-Sanga Island where the plane sometimes arrived on a grassy airstrip built with forced labor during the Japanese occupation. I was returning to Bongao on Tuesday after the third no-show and decided it was time to consider one of the slow, slow ships that lumbered up and down the archipelago. I wasn't looking forward to the long voyage, but it looked like the only way out. The alternative was to brave the seas in one of the even slower and more vulnerable little launches that connected the islands in a lacey network of out-of-the-way ports-of-call. I wasn't ready for that either.

I disembarked the launch at the wharf with other disgruntled would-be passengers and walked down Bongao's only street, prepared to request another night of hospitality at Father Raquet's convento.

"Hey, Americano! I haven't seen you in a long time."

I turned and saw a smiling Tausug man sitting at a table outside the popular seaside bar frequented by the Muslim men who managed to rationalize a few beers into their Islam. "Come and join me and I'll buy you a beer."

"Tabasa! Long time no see. You got yourself a deal." The day was hot and I could think of few things more appealing than a frosty San Miguel at the little bar, the only one in town that sold cold beer. I dropped my bag and fell into the chair beside Tabasa. The plump Christian Filipina who operated the bar brought me a beer and I took a deep swig of it.

"No plane today, eh?" said Tabasa.

"No. The third time. Where you been? I haven't seen you in ages."

"Here and there. Business keeps me on the move." He laughed.

"With a little prodding from the PC?" I suggested.

"That's part of the business game." He laughed again.

Tabasa was in his early forties, tall and solidly built. He was one of Tawi-Tawi's most successful "businessmen," a local euphemism for "smuggler"— not entirely a euphemism because in the eyes of most locals, he was simply participating in the centuries-old trading patterns between Sulawesi, Borneo, and the Sulu Islands. When Europeans carved up island Southeast Asia into the colonies that eventually became nation states, those old trading routes crossed international boundaries and the once legitimate trading practices became smuggling.

"Are you in town for awhile?" I asked.

"Only until tomorrow. I'm going to Zamboanga."

"A business run?"

"Not entirely. I'm taking my cousin's wife to Zamboanga. Her baby's due soon and she wants to be with her mother when it's born."

"How long does it take you to get to Zambo?"

"In good weather I can make it in a long day. The *Ista Bilu* is fast."

"So I've heard." The *Ista Bilu*, a Tausug name meaning "Blue Fish," was one of the fastest smuggling launches in Tawi-Tawi, easily outrunning the patrol boats of the Philippine Navy. "Any chance of taking an additional passenger? I have to be in Manila this weekend. I'm about to give up on planes and I'm not sure when another ship is headed north."

"You don't mind traveling with smugglers?"

"So long as you don't make me walk the plank. Or is that pirates? Besides, I thought you were a businessman."

"It's mostly a personal trip. I have some business in Zamboanga, but mostly I'm making the trip for my cousin. I might be involved in a little business on the way back."

"So when do we leave?"

"About four in the morning. The tide'll be high and we can save some time going over reefs instead of around them."

"Sounds good. Where should I meet you?"

"The Chinese Pier. In front of Bua Ho's store."

"I'll be there."

Four o'clock arrived too early. I can handle early-rising if the sun's up, but I don't like surrendering my mattress in darkness. I crawled out of bed at three-thirty, splashed cold water on my face, pulled on some clothes, grabbed my bag, and stumbled from the convento into the warm darkness. I walked down the street where a few night-market vendors displayed wares for the late nighters and early risers. I left the main thoroughfare for a skinny alley that zigzagged through a motley collection of shacks until I reached Chinese Pier, the commercial heart of Bongao and the wharf for vessels frequenting its marketplace. I found Bua Ho's store, but saw no sign of the *Ista Bilu*. My watch read four, but I'd been in Tawi-Tawi long enough to know that appointments are always approximations. I dropped my bag, sat on a packing crate, and sleepily watched the awakening waterfront. In front of me, a little inter-island launch was secured to the wharf. A small lamp on its deck illuminated the face of a tired old man slowly eating from a bowl of rice. Fishermen in three outriggered boats guarded their boatloads of fish as they awaited the market's opening. Two matronly women arrived with baskets of mangoes, papayas, and a huge jackfruit which they began arranging in displays for anticipated customers. Small waves lapped beneath the pier providing a monotonous but comforting backdrop to the pre-dawn activities. I felt drowsy and was about to doze when a sleek, dark launch quietly approached the pier with *Ista Bilu* written in large white letters on its blue prow.

"Americano!" I recognized Tabasa's voice.

"Hey, Tabasa. Good to see you."

The launch eased to the pier and Tabasa reached out for me. I grabbed his hand, and with a pull from him and a leap from me, I alighted on the deck.

"Our last stop," said Tabasa. "We're on our way." He waved at the man piloting in the cabin at the stern. We reversed from the pier and headed for the channel between Bongao and Sanga-Sanga islands.

I visited the *Ista Bilu* once when it was moored in Bongao, but I'd never been at sea on it. The launch was about thirty feet long, perhaps ten wide at its beam. A small cabin at the stern housed the pilot but the remainder of the deck was open. A canvas awning extended from the pilot house and provided a sheltered space on the deck about eight by twelve feet. The hull was reserved for "business" purposes, mostly American cigarettes smuggled from Borneo to Jolo, Zamboanga, and Manila.

Tabasa was in the cabin with the pilot while I checked out my fellow passengers. A very pretty and very pregnant young woman named Malani rested on a mat beneath the awning with her husband Abi, a young man in his early twenties. An old woman, who I later learned was Malani's aunt, sat beside them. They returned my smile. Leaning over the deck rail was an old man wearing a white turban announcing he'd made the pilgrimage to Mecca. Like the other men, he wore a bolo at his side, the ubiquitous versatile blade of Tawi-Tawi that served as hatchet, knife, and weapon.

I walked to the rail and stood beside the old hajji as the *Ista Bilu* picked up speed. We exchanged silent greetings. The somber peak of Mount Bongao loomed on our port while on starboard Sanga-Sanga's airstrip waited for the planes that wouldn't arrive. Clouds of bats flew above us on their flight home to the caves of Mount Bongao where they would sleep the day preparatory to another night of foraging. Limp-sailed fishing boats paddled by tired fishermen headed for the Bongao market with catches for early shoppers. In an awakening village on the Sanga-Sanga shore, a call to prayer signaled the beginning of another day as red tinged the eastern sky. The engine revved into full throttle and we moved out of the channel into the open sea.

The old hajji and Abi spread mats on the deck, faced west toward Mecca and bowed at their waists murmuring Arabic prayers. They then dropped to their knees, prostrated themselves, and offered additional prayers. Abi concluded his ritual, rolled up his mat, and returned to his wife. The old hajji continued praying, after which he rolled his mat and sat gazing at the sea.

I watched the sunrise. Mornings and evenings were my favorite times at sea. Dawn was a cool respite before the sun climbed higher, raising temperatures and reflecting burning rays from the water's surface. The sunset put an end to the heat, ushering back coolness. The colors of the sunrise were fading when Tabasa joined me at the rail.

"We're heading more westerly than usual," I said.

"You're observant," he smiled. "We're avoiding the usual route. I don't like company."

"And by company, you mean naval patrols?"

"They're not my favorite people."

"I thought you told me this wasn't a 'business' trip."

"I always mix a little business with pleasure. But just in case we're stopped, you don't know that."

"I haven't heard a word."

"We should reach Jolo by mid-afternoon. And if you're lucky, you can catch a plane to Zamboanga this evening."

"Sounds good to me."

He returned to the cabin. I decided to unroll my sleeping mat under the awning and catch up on some of the sleep deprived me the previous night. Malani was lying on a mat with her husband and aunt seated beside her. The old hajji slept on his mat. I sprawled on my mat, shaped my duffle bag into a pillow of sorts, and before long was dozing to the comforting sounds of the *Ista Bilu* slicing through the smooth morning waters.

I'm not sure how long I slept. Perhaps two hours, maybe less. When I awakened the sun was high and heat waves shimmered on the deck beyond the canopy's shade. The young couple and the old aunt were still together on their mats. The hajji leaned over the rail at the bow gazing toward the horizon. The deck was steady and the sea calm. I slowly became aware of the silence that awakened me. The engine was not operating.

Tabasa and the pilot were talking in the cabin. I approached them, curious about what was happening.

"Why have we stopped?" I asked.

"Engine trouble," Tabasa replied. He and the pilot were examining the engine beneath the cabin floor.

"Anything serious?"

"Probably not. It's a new engine. We're trying to figure out what's wrong."

"Where are we? I've been sleeping."

"About an hour west of Siasi." He said something I didn't understand to the pilot peering into the dark recess occupied by the engine. They were obviously preoccupied with mechanical problems and didn't need questions from me so I returned to my mat.

"What's wrong?" Abi asked me.

"I'm not sure. Engine trouble of some sort. They're working on it."

"This is a cursed launch," said the hajji quietly to himself.

"What do you mean?" asked Malani.

"This was the launch of Hajji Muhmad of Zamboanga. The day he bought it, his wife died. Two weeks later, he took his family on a picnic to Sambat Island and his grandson drowned. That's why he sold the launch. It's cursed."

"That's nonsense," said Tabasa, approaching the hajji. "Those things had nothing to do with this launch. Besides after I bought it, an imam blessed it and it was completely rebuilt to accommodate this new engine. It's not the same launch that Hajji Muhmad owned."

"Some curses cannot be removed," said the hajji.

"Nonsense," said Tabasa, dismissively. He returned to the cabin.

"We're far from the main routes," continued the hajji. "No one will find us."

"But we must get to Jolo," said Malani, alarm entering her voice. "My mother is expecting us."

"You're frightening the women," said Abi to the hajji. "The engine will be repaired and we'll soon be on our way."

The hajji unrolled his prayer mat and began his ritual ablutions. As he poured water to cleanse his feet and hands, he suddenly stopped. "We must save the water," he said. "It may be many days before we're found." He stepped onto his mat, murmured his prayers, bowed several times, and prostrated to the west.

Tabasa and the pilot continued working on the engine. Several times, it groaned, coughed, and retreated into silence. I considered the situation. I expected a trip of no more than four or five hours and consequently brought little food and water. I didn't know what the others brought, but they, too, probably had few provisions. We might drift several days before discovered. I'd heard stories of disabled launches at sea for days and even weeks. Some were never found.

As I entertained these worst-case scenarios, Tabasa returned and announced, "We don't know what's wrong with the engine. This is the first time it's caused problems. My cousin Kabana knows the engine and usually pilots, but he was sick today and couldn't come."

"What will happen to us?" cried Malani.

"I told you this launch is cursed," said the hajji.

"The *Ista Bilu* is not cursed," said Tabasa, angrily. "It's simply engine trouble. We'll wait until we're found."

"But we're off the main route," said the hajji. "We won't be found."

Malani sobbed, "My baby will be born at sea. I want to be with my mother." The aunt began weeping also.

"How much food and water do you have?" Tabasa asked.

We told him our supplies, an assortment of dried fish, rice, cassava, bananas, and papayas. We each had a bottle of water. Including the launch's provisions, Tabasa calculated that we had enough sustenance for about five days although the portions would be meager. He collected our food and water.

"But what if help doesn't come?" asked Malani.

"When we don't arrive at Jolo, they'll send a search party for us," said Tabasa.

"But they won't know where to look," said the hajji.

"They'll know where to look," said Tabasa. "If it rains, we'll catch water from the awning. It's important to conserve our energy. Stay under the awning out of the sun. Does anyone have a fishing line?"

We looked at one another. No one had a line.

"We must pray to Allah," said the hajji. He looked at me. "I suppose you do not pray?"

"My prayers are different from yours."

I walked to the front of the launch. The sea was calm and spread quietly in the late afternoon sun, its silence and emptiness somewhat menacing. I looked for an island or a ship on the horizon, but saw nothing.

Tabasa said, "We'll eat before darkness. The generator's not operating so there'll be no lights. I have a pressurized lantern, but it must be saved for emergencies." He parceled food to each of us: a piece of fish, a half cup of rice, a banana, and a cup of water. I wasn't entirely satiated, but I wasn't hungry.

After eating, the hajji again unrolled his mat and prayed toward the setting sun. Malani and Abi lay together. The aunt looked unhappily into the growing darkness. I lay on the open deck, anticipating the first stars of the evening. Tabasa brought a pressurized kerosene lantern from the cabin and said, "We'll stay awake in shifts. If someone hears or sees a boat, he'll light the lantern." He divided the night into five watches and wrote them on slips of paper. Each man drew a slip. My watch began at four a.m. "We'll work on the engine again in the morning. Maybe a ship will see us."

The night was black and the warm moist air hung like a presence above the silent sea. The moon was a skinny silver slice. It was too dark to write in my journal and I wasn't tired enough for sleep. I felt helpless on the disabled vessel, but somehow it didn't distress me. So much of my time in Tawi-Tawi seemed like a movie happening to someone else. This was another scene from that movie. I fell asleep.

I awakened a few hours later with Tabasa's hand gently shaking my shoulder. It was time for my watch. I rubbed sleep from my eyes and sat up. Tabasa handed me the lantern and disappeared. As I was beginning to decipher shapes in the darkness, Malani screamed.

"What is it?" asked the aunt. "Where is the pain?" Malani cried again.

"Is the baby coming?" asked Abi.

"Maybe," said the aunt. "We need a light."

Tabasa appeared and lighted the lantern. Malani lay beside her husband, her face contorted in pain.

"What can we do?" asked Tabasa.

"Do you have cloths?" asked the aunt.

Tabasa spoke to the pilot who went to the cabin.

"You must lie on your back," the aunt told Malani, helping her turn onto her back. The pilot returned with several towels and gave them to the aunt.

"We need a rope for her to pull on," she said. The pilot brought a rope which Abi tied to the rail. They propped Malani against the low wall surrounding the deck and the aunt placed towels beneath her and then sat back and waited.

I walked to the bow, as far from the women as possible. By now the east was colored with the sunrise and as the sky brightened, Tabasa doused the lantern. He then went to the cabin and returned with our morning portions of food. Malani declined hers.

The morning became a very hot day. The *Ista Bilu* lay sweltering and motionless in the glass-like expanses stretching in all directions to the empty distant horizons. We lounged beneath the awning, the sun sapping our energy and the disabled engine sapping our hope. At mid-afternoon, three dolphins discovered our launch, swam around it, skimming the sea surface, and teasing us with their freedom. They soon tired of us and swam away. I stretched out on my mat and napped. When I awakened in late afternoon, soaked in sweat, nothing had changed except Malani's more frequent moans.

Tabasa appeared with a bottle of water and poured a small cup for each of us. A log floated alongside the launch. Water-logged and encrusted with barnacles, it had obviously been at sea a long time. I wondered if someday someone would find the *Ista Bilu* in a similar condition.

Malani's cries punctuated the remainder of the hot afternoon. We watched the sun set with relief, hoping the darkness would bring respite from the heat. Little relief came, however. The air remained heavy and warm, unstirred by the slightest breeze. We sat in the darkness saying little. Above us a tiny sliver of moon provided light that was soon overwhelmed by the emerging stars. We resumed the watch-schedule of the previous night but slept fitfully, awakened throughout the night by Malani's cries.

At dawn the birth was imminent. Abi comforted his wife, placed a stick between her teeth, and urged her to pull the rope. After several sharp cries, she uttered a prolonged wail and the aunt announced the baby was appearing.

"It's here," she said. Then she was quiet.

"Is it a boy or girl?" asked Abi.

"It's a boy."

There was another silence.

"Is it alright?" asked Abi.

The aunt did not reply immediately. Then she said softly, "No. He's dead." She gently placed the tiny body on the mat.

Abi picked up the little corpse, tears streaming down his face. He returned it to the mat and turned to Malani whose pallid face was bereft of emotions.

The aunt said, "We need more cloths. She is bleeding."

"We have no more," said Tabasa. "We'll have to use our clothes."

I pawed through my bag and found three T-shirts and handed them to the aunt. She took them without comment. The others came forward with more garments.

"The dead baby cannot remain in the boat," said Tabasa. "It will bring bad luck."

"Tabasa is right. It cannot remain on board," said the hajji. "We must give it to the sea." He looked at Abi who glanced at his wife and murmured to her. Her eyes were closed and she didn't respond. Abi looked up and said, "Yes. My son must go to the sea. Allah will take his soul to heaven."

The old hajji dipped water from the sea with a pot attached to a rope. He bathed the dead infant and chanted Arabic prayers to Allah and Sinama prayers to the ancestors. He then wrapped the little corpse in one of my white T-shirts. While the old woman attended to Malani, the hajji spread a mat and lay the infant with its head toward the west. He bowed, dropped on his knees, and offered more prayers. He then moved aside and each of us followed his example. I knelt on the mat and silently reflected on the little boy who would never experience life. Then the aunt approached the tiny corpse and offered her prayers.

The hajji carried the corpse to the prow and held it over the sea in his outstretched arms. He said more prayers and dropped it. A gentle splash disturbed the still waters.

Abi held his semi-conscious wife in his arms while the old woman pulled blood-soaked cloths from under her sarong and inserted fresh ones. The hajji approached and sat beside her.

"This is not good," the aunt said to him. "There should not be blood like this."

"This boat is cursed," said the hajji. "Only Allah can help us."

I stood at the prow searching the empty sea for a ship, an island, anything.

Shortly after midnight, Malani died. I was awake.

The old aunt had tried desperately to stop the flow of blood that now stained the mats and deck. I sat at the bow providing the sad little party as much privacy as possible. The night was moonless but the lantern illuminated the deck.

"She's gone," said the aunt.

Abi said nothing.

"She's gone," repeated the aunt.

Abi released his wife and slowly crawled toward the bow. He sat opposite me, curled into a fetal position. The old hajji murmured a litany of Arabic prayers to Allah and then switched to Sinama for the ancestors. The aunt slowly, carefully, covered Malani's body with a sarong. Then she joined the old man in prayer, tears streaming down her tired old face.

I remained at the bow. Tabasa and his pilot came from the cabin and stood quietly, awkwardly watching the old couple pray. They then offered their own prayers.

Overhead, clouds opened and brought more light to the night.

Suddenly Abi screamed. He stood and screeched, his eyes popping, the veins on his neck bulging and his fists clenched tightly on his rigid arms. He fell to the deck screaming, flailing his arms, and kicking his feet. We all watched, understanding that his loss warranted such an outburst.

He jumped up and began kicking the rail of the deck, beating it with his fists. He grabbed a pole supporting the canvas awning, causing its collapse. At that point, Tabasa and the pilot tried to subdue him. He resisted, kicking and breaking from their grasp, his screams unabated. They pulled him to the deck as his screams dissolved into guttural sobs, tears streaming down his contorted face. His subduers slowly released him and he cried loudly to the empty night with the old woman's muffled sobs providing accompaniment. Abi stopped crying and lay quietly on the deck. The old aunt stopped sobbing, too. Silence returned. The splash of the sea against the *Ista Bilu* offered the only sound.

After many minutes of silence, the hajji said to no one in particular, "We must prepare the body."

More minutes of silence followed before the aunt said, "I will use sea water."

Tabasa went to the cabin and returned with a pot attached to a rope and an empty five-gallon tin. He lowered the pot into the sea and filled the tin. He carried it to the aunt and retreated. The hajji murmured Arabic and Sinama prayers as the aunt spoke quietly to the spirit of the corpse she bathed. She wrapped the body in a sarong and with the assistance of the hajji, encased it in a mat and moved it to the center of the deck.

Abi remained silent, again curled in a fetal position against the rail, saying nothing. No tears, no sobs.

The hajji spoke to Tabasa who then went to the cabin and returned with a small bowl containing a smoldering piece of incense. I joined the little group encircling the corpse. The old hajji invited Abi to join us, but he remained silent and did not move.

The hajji asked the ancestors to accept Malani's spirit and not blame us for we had done all we could to save her. Then each of us recited Malani's admirable traits, filled with flattery and hyperbole so her spirit would not feel slighted and return to haunt us. The hajji again asked Abi to join us, but he remained silent and immobile.

After another prayer, the hajji announced, "We must give the body to the sea. I have told her spirit that we cannot bury her with her ancestors, but she has joined them. Her spirit knows the body cannot be kept on the boat. It will bring a greater curse to us."

"How could the curse be greater?" the aunt cried to herself.

"Abi," said the hajji. "We must give the body to the sea."

Abi said nothing.

At the hajji's instructions, we each offered a final prayer. Then the hajji, Tabasa, the pilot, and I lifted the body, carried it to the railing, and slid it over the side. A splash broke the stillness.

We re-formed our circle on the deck and the hajji offered additional prayers to Allah. Tabasa and the pilot retreated to the cabin. The hajji, the aunt, and I found private spaces on the deck. Abi still did not move.

I lay on the hard deck, drained and exhausted by the events of the night. Soon I heard the soft snores of the old man and the old woman, and then I, too, drifted to sleep.

I cannot detail the horror of the following morning. The memory of that discovery is still too awful and vivid in my memory. I was awakened by the old woman's screams. I sat up startled. The hajji awakened too. Tabasa and the pilot rushed from the cabin. The old woman stood over Abi, screaming hysterically. Abi lay dead in a pool of blood. Sometime during the night, he had plunged his bolo into his stomach.

Only a few hours after we mourned Malani's death, we administered the same rites to her husband. His body was bathed, prayers were offered, and he was given to the sea. We doused the deck with buckets of seawater, but the blood stains of the young family would not wash away.

The next day we bobbed in the open sea, huddled under the awning and inside the cabin to escape the merciless sun. On the second day, a rain squall brought a brief respite. We saw it coming and adjusted the canopy to funnel the rain into the containers we readied to capture it. Later, five flying fish landed on the deck, adding to our food supply.

We talked little during those days. Tabasa and the pilot periodically attempted to start the engine, but they eventually admitted they knew nothing about engines. We did not speak of the deaths. It was unnecessary. The blood stains on the deck were constant reminders.

On the third day we spotted a ship on the horizon. We shouted until our throats hurt, waved everything we could find, fired a gun, and lighted the lantern. All to no avail. The ship didn't see us, or chose not to. It disappeared over the horizon.

The next day a plane passed overhead. We screamed and waved, but again to no avail.

I began to realize that I might die on the *Ista Bilu*.

The following morning ushered in a day without a breath of wind, another scorcher that sizzled us on the glassy quiet sea. We had consumed our midmorning allotment of water when suddenly the old hajji shouted, "A launch! Straight to the south! A launch!"

We all rushed to him and looked in the direction he was pointing. Sure enough, a launch was visible in the southern sea. And more important, it was heading toward us. We each grabbed something to wave. The hajji tied a yellow shirt to a long pole and waved it. I waved my T-shirt from another pole. The pilot lighted the lantern, hoping it might send a signal through the bright sun. Tabasa considered firing into the air but reconsidered, thinking it might frighten the launch away. It continued toward us, apparently having seen us.

"I wonder why they're stopping for us," said Tabasa.

"Who cares?" I said. "Be glad it's coming."

"They probably saw our flags," suggested the aunt, "and knew we were in trouble."

"It was headed toward us before it could've seen our flags," said Tabasa. "It may be pirates."

"Who cares who they are," I said. "Just so they help us."

"They'll take my cargo," said Tabasa.

"We'll give it to them if they'll take us to land," said the aunt.

The launch bore rapidly toward us. We could now distinguish its green hull and a lone figure at the prow.

"I don't trust it," said Tabasa. He tucked a revolver into his belt and pulled his loose shirt over it. He spoke to the pilot who hurried to the cabin and returned with an automatic rifle that he placed in a recess at the prow.

The hajji continued waving the yellow shirt at the approaching launch.

"Do you recognize it?" I asked Tabasa.

"No," he said. "I've never seen a launch like that in Tawi-Tawi. It looks like a Buginese boat."

When the launch was about a hundred yards from us, it reduced its speed.

"We're adrift," shouted Tabasa. "Can you help us?"

No response came from the launch as it slowly approached us. The man at the prow stood motionless. When the vessel was about a hundred feet away, it stopped and the man shouted to us.

"What did he say?" I asked, unable to hear him.

"I'm not sure," said Tabasa. "I think it was Indonesian."

Tabasa shouted back in Indonesian. I knew enough of the language to understand that he was telling him we needed help.

The launch drew nearer and another man appeared on deck. "We have guns," he said, brandishing an automatic rifle. "But we'll not shoot if you cooperate."

"We need your help," shouted the hajji. "In the name of Allah, please help us. We've been adrift a week and three of us have died." Our communication became a mixture of English, Indonesian, and Tausug. Somehow it worked.

Three more men appeared on deck, also armed. They spoke among themselves and aimed their guns toward us as their boat moved closer.

"I knew it. They're pirates," muttered Tabasa.

"If you have guns, throw them on deck where we can see them."

Tabasa and the pilot did not move.

"Do as they say," said the hajji. "We must trust in merciful Allah that they'll spare us."

"Yes," said the aunt. "Do as they say."

Tabasa looked at each of us and then shouted in Indonesian, "We have only two guns. We'll place them on the deck." He took his revolver from his belt and tossed it on the deck. He nodded to the pilot who retrieved the rifle from its hiding place and placed it beside the revolver.

"We're coming aboard," said the man who initially addressed us, apparently the ringleader. "Don't attempt to stop us or we'll kill you."

"We beg your mercy," cried the aunt. "We'll die if you don't help us."

The men ignored her and boarded the *Ista Bilu*, their guns pointed at us.

"Is anyone else aboard?" asked the leader.

"No," said Tabasa. "We are only five now."

"Who's the white man?"

"An American. A passenger. He lives in Tawi-Tawi."

"What's your cargo?"

Tabasa did not respond.

"Don't lie. We'll soon find out."

"We have cigarettes from Sabah. We're taking them to Zamboanga."

"They're his, not ours," said the aunt. "We're only passengers."

"All of you move to starboard," said the leader.

We did as ordered. Two of the men kicked the guns on the deck behind them and stood with their own guns aimed at us. The other two went into the cabin and entered the hold. They returned with five large cardboard crates and stacked them on the deck.

"Are you carrying anything else? Don't lie because we'll search more. This is a small cargo."

"That's all I have," said Tabasa. "I was taking my cousin and her husband to Jolo where she could have her baby. But she and the baby died and her husband killed himself."

"Have pity on us," cried the aunt. "We've suffered enough. We are fellow Muslims—except this heathen American. Allah will bless you if you help us."

The leader spoke to his men and they returned to the hold. We heard their voices as they searched further.

"That's my only cargo," said Tabasa. The leader looked at him and said nothing.

Several minutes later the other two men emerged from below with two five-gallon tins of gasoline. The leader spoke to them and they transferred the cigarettes and gasoline to their launch.

"Where are we?" asked Tabasa. "We've been drifting for a week and have no idea where we are."

"You're near Usada Island."

"Can you tow us there? We've cooperated with you. We've given you our cargo."

"We *took* your cargo. You wouldn't have given it if we had no guns."

"You cannot leave fellow Muslims to die in the open sea," said the hajji. "We have suffered so much already."

The leader looked at him steadily for several moments and then spoke briefly to his companions. He said, "We'll pull you toward Usada. We can't take you all the way, but maybe we'll meet a boat that will help you."

"May Allah bless you and your families all the days of your life," said the aunt, dropping to her knees.

The leader ignored her and spoke to a man aboard his launch. He disappeared and returned with a heavy rope and tossed it to the *Ista Bilu* where one of his companions secured it. Two of the pirates remained aboard our launch while the others returned to their vessel and slowly towed us eastward.

About twenty minutes later, someone shouted that Usada was straight ahead. Never had an island looked so good to me. But looking even better was a fishing boat sailing toward us. When it approached, the pirates told the fishermen that our launch was disabled and they could not tow us further. They returned to their launch, untied the towrope, and sped away.

"May Allah bless you! May Allah bless you!" cried the hajji.

"May Allah curse you bastards for taking my cigarettes," muttered Tabasa. He called to the fishermen, "We're having engine trouble. Can you take us to Usada?"

"We only have room for one of you," said the older of the two fishermen.

"I'll come with you," said Tabasa. "Is there a launch at Usada that can tow us?"

"Yes. My cousin has a launch." The fishermen approached the *Ista Bilu* and Tabasa climbed down, promising to return as soon as possible. Within an hour, he was back with a launch and within another hour, we arrived at Usada's little wharf where the entire village awaited us, having heard our story from Tabasa. We scrambled from the *Ista Bilu*, eager to abandon the ill-fated vessel.

Unsurprisingly, the aunt and the hajji had relatives in the village, unsurprising because of the web of kinship that connects the scattered islands of Tawi-Tawi. The old aunt hugged a distant cousin and wailed as she related our tragic voyage. Other women joined her wail and several men wept, too. The children, however, were more interested in the strange-looking white man than the *Ista Bilu* and stared openly at me, the more brazen touching me to see if I was real. The aunt luridly recounted the details of our tragedy. I'm certain she was genuinely grieved by the deaths of her relatives, but she was nonetheless relishing her central role in the events.

The hajji decided a thanksgiving ceremony was in order. All of us from the *Ista Bilu* plus several village elders sat in a circle with a plate of fish and rice, a coconut, and a glass of water in the center, the traditional offerings to ancestral spirits. Incense was lighted to attract the spirits and prayers of thanks were offered to them. When the ceremony concluded, the village imam suggested we go to the mosque for a thanksgiving service to Allah. I wasn't sure how I would be accommodated as a non-Muslim, but their only concern was I didn't have a prayer cap. That was soon resolved when an old man came forward with a cap he retrieved from a trunk in a corner of the room. We walked to the mosque, bathed our feet, and entered. After the service, we returned to the imam's house where food awaited. I ate tentatively and then greedily, my stomach reminding me I'd eaten little during the past week.

We stayed at the hospitable little village for two nights. On the early morning of the third day, a launch transported us to Siasi and from there I caught another launch to Jolo. Later that evening, I was on a flight to Manila.

But that's not the end of the story of the *Ista Bilu*. The launch was sold and completely refurbished by its new owner. About six months after our fateful voyage, it departed Bongao on its maiden voyage to Manado across the Sulawesi Sea. It was never seen again. Official investigations concluded that it was either destroyed in a storm or captured by pirates. Perhaps, said the local people, but whatever happened, the curse of the *Ista Bilu* was responsible.

The tragedy of the *Ista Bilu* eventually passed into Tawi-Tawi lore. Balladeers fashioned it into a long ballad which is still sung throughout the islands. Stories abound about ship captains who occasionally hear inexplicable human sounds at sea during dark, misty nights which some believe are the cries of the dead baby, the moans of the dying Malani, or the desperate screams of Abi. And every fisherman knows-a-fisherman-who-knows-a-fisherman who encountered the shadowy form of the barnacle-clad *Ista Bilu* in the dead of night emitting muffled cries of pain and anguish.

And I, after all these years, still sometimes start from a sound sleep with images of that dreadful voyage drifting through my disturbed dreams.

The Expat

E xpats are a mixed bag. Until I met a few I
thought they were all romantic malcontents
melancholically seeking answers to life's
perplexing questions in exotic faraway places.
Probably some of them fit that stereotype, but
most don't. Many live overseas simply because
their jobs dictate it and they are as pedestrian overseas as
they were back home. Some of the white ones like the
post-colonial status they still enjoy in former colonies where
they live a lifestyle they could never afford at home. A few
altruistic souls genuinely believe they can ease the ills of the
world by charitably tackling medical and social problems in
disadvantaged countries. Some simply don't like the cultures
they were born into. Others have been so maimed and broken
by their natal cultures that they seek another one for solace
while healing their wounds. Maybe Mister Bob was the latter
type. I'm not sure. He was a strange mix.

I met Mister Bob one day when I was wandering around
Jolo. I was taking a break from Tawi-Tawi and its distractions

in order to wrap up a paper I was writing. I was staying at a boarding house I patronized while in town and had finished lunch when I decided to take a stroll around town. Sometime ago I discovered that few things were more entertaining than wandering the streets and alleys of Jolo, the bustling energetic capital of the Sulu Archipelago.

Back in those days before the secessionist battles of the 1970s left it in shambles, Jolo was a lively town filled with all sorts of sounds, smells, colors, and people. Brightly decorated jeepneys and pedicabs honked and shouted their way through the colorful crowds that crammed and clogged its thoroughfares. An endless stream of ships, launches, and sailboats moved in and out of its busy harbor. And in the heart of it all was the marketplace where one could spend days and still never see all it offered to shoppers. It was a tightly packed little town, most residents reluctant to wander too far beyond its boundaries because of real and imagined dangers in the hinterland. I joined the lively sea that flooded its streets to see where the currents would take me.

It was a hot day, of course. All days in Jolo seemed hot. Most locals were taking siestas to escape the hottest part of the day but I, like the proverbial mad dogs and Englishmen, chose the midday sun for my stroll around town. I turned from the main thoroughfare and entered a little alley that soon became a cul-de-sac. I spotted an engine repair shop and decided to explore it, partly because I'd never seen such a shop in the islands. The smells of gasoline and oil overwhelmed me when I entered. As I adjusted my eyes to the dark interior, I was surprised to see a Caucasian man dressed in denim coveralls, slim, rather nondescript, and probably in his mid-forties, working on an engine with a Tausug assistant. The Tausug man smiled at me, but the other man only looked at me briefly and continued working.

Undaunted, I approached him and said, "Good afternoon."

He smiled slightly, not looking up from the engine he was repairing.

The Tausug man said, "Good afternoon."

"Is this your shop?" I asked him.

"It's my brother-in-law's shop." He nodded toward the white man.

"Are you an American?" I asked the white man.

"Yes," he said. "But I have work to do." He walked away and entered a back room.

The Tausug man looked embarrassed and said, "I'm sorry, but he's very shy."

"I didn't mean to intrude."

"It's alright."

I left the shop, blinked my way into the bright sunshine, and resumed my wandering.

That evening after dinner I sat with Mrs. Mabun on her balcony overlooking Jolo's main thoroughfare. A Christian Filipina married to a Muslim man, she operated the boarding house where I was staying. We were drinking cool glasses of *kalamansi* juice while digesting one of her great dinners. Mrs. Mabun was telling me about the approaching mayoral race when a pause entered our conversation. I remembered the American man I saw that afternoon and decided to see what she knew about him.

"I met a strange American man this afternoon," I began.

"That can only be one man," she interrupted. "There's only one American man in Jolo who isn't a priest and he's certainly strange. You must have met Mister Bob."

"He's a mechanic."

She laughed. "Yes, that's Mister Bob. He's a very good mechanic, but he's a strange one. He lives alone. Some people think he's possessed by a *saitan*. Did he talk to you?"

"Not a lot. Mister Bob? Is that his name?"

"That's what everyone calls him. He hardly talks to anyone. Some call him 'The Music Man.'"

"Why is that?"

"He likes to listen to that old-fashioned music."

"Have you ever talked to him?"

"Once. My sister took her car to him for repairs and I went with her to pick it up. I tried to talk to him, but he only said a few words and then made an excuse to leave. He's an odd one."

She stood. "I must turn down the beds before the other guests return. If you're finished, I'll take your glass."

That evening the moon was full and the night pleasantly cool so I decided to walk to a beach at the edge of town I sometimes visited when in Jolo. I met a few people along the way, but for the most part I was alone enjoying the solitude that the busy little city denied me. I reached the beach and sat in the still warm sand. It was a storybook night, the sort that inspired tropical clichés. Swaying palm fronds framed the full moon's reflection on the sparkling rippling waters of a high tide. Only the lap of small breakers and the gentle rattling of fronds provided sound. I lay back propped on my elbows enjoying the quiet night when piano music slowly entered the darkness. At first I thought my imagination was adding more romance to the already romantic night. But it was not my imagination. The improbable but unmistakable strains of Beethoven's *Moonlight Sonata* drifted through the warm moonlight. I savored the sonata several minutes, but as much as I was enjoying it, I was also curious to know where it was coming from. A small house with muted light falling from its windows stood alone at the edge of the beach. I walked toward it. Sure enough, it was the source of the music. I sat on a large rock outside the house and listened to the remaining sonata. It ended and the night was quiet again.

A man wearing a sarong and T-shirt stepped from the house onto the lanai, stretched his arms upward, and looked toward the beach. Then he saw me.

"Who are you?" he asked loudly and somewhat suspiciously.

"I'm sorry," I said. "I didn't mean to intrude, but I heard your music and stopped to listen. It's very beautiful."

"Who are you?" he asked again. He turned and the light caught his face. I recognized the man I'd met earlier at the engine repair shop.

"We met this afternoon. I'm the American who visited your shop." I approached him. "We share a taste in music."

"You like that kind of music?" he asked cautiously.

"Yes, I do. May I join you?"

He hesitated and then said, "Okay." He sat in a chair on the lanai.

"May I sit?"

He glanced at me hesitantly and said, "I guess it's okay."

I sat beside him. "Was the music from your radio?" I knew of no radio station in the islands, but occasionally some of the stronger radios picked up *The Voice of America*. Perhaps he had such a radio.

"No. I have records. Would you like to hear more music?"

"Yes, very much."

He stood. "You stay out here. I'll go inside. I don't like interruptions when I listen to the music."

"I'll be quiet."

He entered the house and minutes later the music began again, this time the unmistakable first movement of Dvorak's *New World Symphony*. I leaned back in the chair, closed my eyes, and traveled with the music to that place where music goes. Too soon, the symphony concluded but it was several minutes before Mister Bob appeared at the door and announced, "It's time for me to go to bed."

"Thanks for sharing your music. It's been a long time since I've heard any like it."

He did not immediately respond and then said, "I play music every night." He hesitated. "I suppose it's okay if you want to stop by and listen."

"That's very generous of you. I'd like that very much. What's a good time?"

"I usually begin about seven."

I thanked him again and told him I'd stop by the following evening. I returned to the beach and sat in the sand enjoying more of the night.

The next evening I walked to Mister Bob's house. He appeared at the door when I stepped onto the lanai. "Good evening," I said. "And thanks again for inviting me."

"You can come inside."

I entered a sparsely furnished room. A record player sat atop a table at one end. Beside it a crude bookcase held a couple dozen

LPs carefully spaced, probably to minimize the tropical mold and mildew. A lounge chair and a single bed completed the furnishings. A dim floor lamp provided the only illumination. I heard a noise in a corner and was surprised to see a very curious little brown monkey sitting in a small bed staring at me.

"You have a pet monkey."

He looked at the monkey and said, "Sometimes he comes here at night."

"What's his name?"

He looked at me puzzled and then said, "I don't know. 'Monkey,' I guess. I found him on the lanai when he was a baby. I fed him and he stayed around. Sit in the chair. I don't talk when the music is playing."

"I understand."

I sat as instructed and he went to the bookcase, pulled out an LP, and placed it on the turntable. The needle dropped to the vinyl and the most familiar four notes in Western classical music announced the opening of Beethoven's *Fifth Symphony*. Mister Bob lay on his bed with closed eyes. I found a comfortable position in my chair and listened to the symphony I knew so well but hadn't heard in many months. I, too, closed my eyes. Too soon the symphony ended and I sat quietly waiting for Mister Bob to terminate the silence. "You can talk now," he said.

I tried to think of a harmless subject and came up with, "Where did you learn about engines?"

He looked at me blankly a couple of moments and then said, "I don't know. I always liked them, even when I was a little kid. The old man had a Model A Ford. He was always fixing it. I watched him work on it. Engines are easy. Once you understand them they're easy to fix. No one here knew about engines when I first came. There weren't many around. When more jeepneys and launches began arriving, they brought them to me to fix. I had a good business. Me and my brother-in-law still do."

He was quiet again. I prodded the conversation: "How long you been married?"

"I'm not married no more." He was silent. "She died."

"I'm sorry."

He looked at me and shrugged. "She was okay, but I didn't like her all that much. We had a kid. She's with her grandparents. I give them money and they leave me alone. I never see her. I don't like kids much."

"Don't you get lonely?"

"No." He was silent again and then said, "You mean this?" He moved his index finger up and down in his closed fist.

"That too."

"A *bantut* comes around. Takes care of me and makes him happy too. He'd probably do you if you're interested."

"Thanks, but I'm okay."

He shrugged.

It was several months before I saw Mister Bob again. I was returning from Manila where I bought some LPs for him and stopped in Jolo to deliver them. When I entered his repair shop, he looked up from the engine he was repairing and offered a weak smile.

"Good to see you again," I said.

He murmured a greeting and continued working. "I'll be playing music tonight if you want to stop by."

"I'd like that. See you at seven."

A light mist was falling when I arrived at Mister Bob's house. As I stepped onto his lanai and called his name, a breeze rattled the surrounding palm fronds. He invited me inside.

"I brought you some LPs from Manila," I said, handing them to him.

"Oh. Okay." He seemed embarrassed as he reached out to accept them. Monkey awakened from his bed in the corner, gave me a few curious blinks, and shut his eyes again.

Mister Bob placed the LPs on the table without looking at them. He nodded me toward my chair and placed an LP on the turntable. Tchaikovsky's *First Piano Concerto* began the evening's concert. He went to his bed and stretched out.

Monkey awoke during the concerto and sat quietly in his bed watching me, occasionally scratching an itch. When the music ended, Mister Bob said we could talk.

"It's a very beautiful concerto," I said unoriginally. He said nothing. I continued, "Have you liked classical music all your life?"

"No." He didn't elaborate.

The conversation was going nowhere, so I tried a different tack. "What part of the States are you from?"

"Oklahoma. I'm an Oakie who made it to California. You heard of the Dust Bowl? We left it."

"I'm from California too. Is your family still there?"

"Probably. I haven't seen them in years."

"Do you have siblings?"

"What are siblings?" He looked everywhere except at me when he talked.

"Brothers and sisters."

He thought quietly for a moment and then surprised me with a torrent of more than I wanted to know. "Eight. Maybe Ma had some more. Maybe some of them died. I don't know. I hated the old man. Never any money for food. We were always hungry. I haven't seen any of them since I left. And I don't want to see them."

"When did you leave home?"

"Home? Is that what you call it?" He laughed. "Long time ago. Maybe a year after we got to California. I went up to Oakland. Lived there a few years and joined the army. Lied about my age. I was tired of being hungry and no place to sleep." He stood and walked to the record player. He removed the LP from the turntable and replaced it with Shostakovich's *Fifth Symphony*.

After it ended, I asked him when he first heard classical music.

"On the radio, when I was in the army. The base had a few records. Only one other guy liked them. He was killed."

"I'm sorry. Was he your friend?"

He shrugged. "I never had a friend." He paused. "Once I had sort of a friend. A Filipino doctor here in Jolo. One day he heard me listening to music on the radio and said he'd give me some LPs and a record player if I'd fix his car. He moved to Manila. Sometimes he sends me LPs."

"I could come by in the daytime if that would work better for you."

"No. I only listen to music at night. It means nothing in the daytime. It must be dark." He put the LP in its jacket and returned it to the shelf. "I'm going to bed now."

I thanked him and took my leave.

The next evening I returned to Mister Bob's house with some beer and Cokes. When I offered them to him, he told me he didn't drink anything but water. I set them aside as he readied the record player. We quietly listened to Ravel's *Bolero* ascend to its orgasmic climax after which he announced that it was okay to talk.

"Where's Monkey?" I asked. The small bed in the corner was empty.

"I don't know. He doesn't come every night."

I watched him return the LP to the shelf and then asked, "How did you end up in the Philippines?"

"An older guy in my barracks spent time here. He was always talking about the palm trees and beaches and how it's warm all the time. How friendly the people are. I liked the way it sounded. I came right after I was discharged. Manila looked like what I left in Germany. Like a huge bomb fell on it. I didn't want any more of that, but I didn't have enough money to go back to the States. Anyway, I didn't want to go back there."

"Why did you come down here?"

"It was far away from Manila—and the States. And Germany."

"You were in Germany during the war?"

"Yeah. Fighting the Krauts. You ever heard of a place called Dachau?" He didn't wait for an answer. "I was with the troops that liberated Dachau." He paused. "You probably seen the pictures and newsreels, but they don't begin to tell the story. You need to hear the cries and whimpering and smell those smells. See those skinny little kids. See the ones who couldn't say anything." He stopped.

I said nothing, not sure if he wanted to continue.

He did. "The Krauts knew they couldn't stop us so they surrendered. The place was littered with bodies. An entire train was filled with dead people. We thought we'd rounded up all the Kraut soldiers, but one of the prisoners pointed to a railroad car. Me and three other guys went to the car and pulled open the door. Six Krauts were inside. They threw down their guns and held up their hands. We looked at them several minutes and then someone said, 'Do these butchers deserve to live?' It was an easy one to answer. We opened fire and killed them all. They were defenseless—just like all those Jews they murdered. But we killed them all. I wish we could've killed more." He looked at me for the first time that evening. "You probably think it's awful—killing surrendered enemy combatants. Maybe it is. Who cares? Those butchers deserved to die."

I had nothing to offer.

"When we returned to camp, no one asked about those Krauts we shot. They didn't care. They'd killed their own share. Some of the prisoners beat the guards to death with shovels, sticks, anything. We stayed there about a week trying to help the ones still alive. Watching them die like flies. Burying all those bodies in big holes. The stink was everywhere. You couldn't get away from it. I hate Krauts." He stopped. "I don't want to talk about it anymore."

He walked to the record player and selected an LP. I recognized the overture to Wagner's *Tannhäuser*.

Two weeks later I was aboard the *Zamboanga Star*, one of the slow Chinese cargo ships that plodded up and down the Sulu

Archipelago. We wended around and above reefs, skirted tiny islands, passed fishermen in outriggers, and entered an inky tropical night. I stretched out on the upper deck with the stars above me and the reassuring throb of the engine beneath me and on the cot beside me Father Raquet who was on his way home from a conference in Jolo. As we silently watched the stars above, I remembered Mister Bob. "Do you know the American man in Jolo named Mister Bob?"

"Of course, I do. Everyone in Jolo knows Mister Bob. Or I should say knows about him. I don't think anyone really knows him."

"Have you ever talked to him?"

"Yes, long ago. After the war. I think he was looking for his island paradise in Tawi-Tawi. He stayed with me a few days. We talked about the war, of course. I think he arrived in Manila shortly after the war ended. Manila was almost leveled. It was probably still pretty much a war zone when he arrived."

"He told me it looked like some of the places he saw in Germany."

"I remember him as rather vague and vacant. Didn't have a lot to say. He certainly didn't have much good to say about the Germans, but no one did back then. He never wanted to talk about the war, so I stopped asking him about it. He told me he was with the D-Day invasion, but he never said much more. He must have seen some brutal fighting."

"He told me he was with the troops that liberated Dachau."

"He never mentioned that to me. Poor fellow. D–Day and Dachau. No wonder he's odd. I sensed he was very broken by the war. Like a lot of men."

"Do you know how he made it to Tawi–Tawi?"

"He once told me he was looking for a warm place with no white people. I think he fought in some bitter winters in Europe and had no love for Europeans and their war. He stayed with me about a week, but I think he was in Tawi–Tawi a couple of years."

"Really? That long? Where was he all that time?"

"You know that little island called La`a? It was uninhabited at the time. Maybe it still is. He built a house there, apparently not knowing someone claimed the island. Eventually the datu who owned the place decided it was time for him to move on. He found another island. I don't remember the name of it, somewhere over by Tandubas. Same thing happened. After a few months, he was told to leave. That's when he went to Jolo."

"I wonder why he went to Jolo. It's not exactly an isolated tropical island."

"Maybe he decided that life on an isolated tropical island isn't what it's cracked up to be. Maybe he got lonely." He was quiet several moments. "We humans are strange creatures. We have trouble getting along with one another, yet we can't live alone."

Mister Bob was one of the least curious persons I've ever known. During my visits to his home, he never once asked me a personal question. He was uninterested in where I was from, where I'd been, or what I was doing in the Philippines. I'm not even sure he knew my name.

Ironically, his disinterest also extended to the music he seemed to love. When I asked him about his favorite composers, he looked blank and said he didn't know their names and only knew the music by the pictures on the LP jackets. He said he liked them all—although he once told me a Mozart recording was not serious enough. He'd never read the discussions on the backs of the LP jackets. I wondered how well he could read. He didn't know the difference between a symphony, a sonata, and a concerto. He told me he hated opera after I explained to him what it was. He heard arias on *The Voice of America* once and said he couldn't stand the screeching.

For someone who'd lived in Jolo almost twenty years, he knew little about the local culture and had no interest in learning more. He obviously knew a great deal about engines, but absolutely no interest in talking about them or why he found them interesting—if in fact he did. He never owned a vehicle.

I never saw anyone at Mister Bob's house except Monkey. He once told me a housekeeper prepared his evening meals, but I never saw her.

I was on my way out of the Philippines when I last saw Mister Bob. I'd finished my research in Tawi-Tawi and stopped at Jolo to wrap up some loose ends and say goodbye to people I knew there, including Mister Bob. I arrived with a monsoon storm.

It was the second day of the rains and I was tired of the confinement of Mrs. Mabun's boarding house. After dinner, I found an umbrella and headed toward Mister Bob's place, unsure whether the inclement weather would interfere with his nightly music. The wind soon whipped my umbrella into uselessness as I skirted puddles and fallen fronds with the wind howling around me. By the time I reached Mister Bob's house, I was soaked. He came to the door and murmured "Hi" after I shouted my arrival. He seemed unsurprised to see me and offered no towel or dry clothes. I sat in my usual chair and he placed an LP on the turntable. Monkey sat in his bed eating a mango. He was wet, apparently having been outside. I recognized the beginning of a Mahler symphony. Mister Bob cranked up the volume until the music drowned out the howling night. When the symphony ended, the sounds of the storm returned.

For several minutes we said nothing, listening to the rain pound the metal roof and the wind roar through the trees. Occasionally the sounds of restless surf joined the cacophony.

Finally I said, "I'm leaving the Philippines."

"Oh. Why?"

"I finished my research. I'm going back to the States."

"Oh. Okay." He was silent several moments and then said, "When will you come back?"

"I'm not sure, but it'll probably be a long time." More silence. "I've enjoyed our evenings together and I want to thank you for sharing your music with me. I greatly appreciate it."

"Yes," he said, tightly.

Several more silent awkward moments passed. "I must go now."

I held out my hand for a farewell shake. He glanced at my hand and looked at me, one of the few times he ever looked into my eyes. "You're the only friend I've ever had." He pressed my hand quickly and returned to the record player with his back toward me. "You'd better go now."

I looked at him, not knowing what to say. Monkey sat in his bed watching us. After several more awkward moments, I picked up my disabled umbrella and returned to the storm outside. I walked away from the house into the swirling wet darkness as the swells of Beethoven's *Ninth Symphony* joined the noises of the night.

Departure

During my early months in Tawi-Tawi, I thought I would never want to leave the islands. Life was idyllic in my little boat sailing above colorful coral reefs among tropical islands. I awakened to spectacular sunrises. During the days when I wasn't with the Sama Dilaut, I explored uninhabited islets, waded pools of the low tide, and wandered deserted white sand beaches. Kaleidoscopic sunsets concluded my days. I slept beneath the cycles of the moon, back-dropped by billions of stars. The sea was filled with fish for my taking and the islands provided whatever additional sustenance I needed. My drinking water often came from the sky or from a coconut on one of the scores of islands that dotted my seascape. Much of the world fantasized the life I was living and I was always aware how special and unique my experience was, not only in terms of the anthropological data I was collecting, but more important, the personal journey I was undertaking.

But as the months progressed, the romance began to fade. Tawi-Tawi didn't change, I did. I increasingly realized that, like it or not, I was a creature of my own culture and I began to miss that culture, flawed though I perceived it. Toward the end I was ambivalent about leaving, but I knew it was time to go. My adventure had played itself out, my research was completed, and I was ready for the next chapter of my life.

I initially planned to leave on one of the slow cargo ships that lumbered up and down the archipelago, thinking the leisurely journey would provide an easier transition to my next chapter. But in the end, I changed my mind and decided to make my departure abrupt. The Sama Dilaut had no farewell party. That was not their way. Masa and his family quietly watched me board an airplane near their Sanga-Sanga moorage with my field notes and memories. I flew up the archipelago toward Zamboanga, fighting tears, and watching the familiar islands drop behind me one by one, not knowing those islands were on the verge of catastrophic change.

Shortly after I left, a civil war erupted in the southern Philippines as Muslim separatists pushed for an independent Islamic state. That conflict is ongoing and its many ramifications are far beyond this discussion, but most significantly for Tawi-Tawi, it resulted in large numbers of refugees fleeing the northern islands for the relative peace of Tawi-Tawi. At about this same time, seaweed aquaculture was introduced to the sprawling Tawi-Tawi reefs, the traditional home of the Sama Dilaut. This new industry brought even more outsiders, many displacing the Sama Dilaut. Meanwhile, Tawi-Tawi became a separate province from the rest of the Sulu Archipelago and this attracted outside administrators, peace keepers, and entrepreneurs. And while all this was happening, a more fundamentalist Islam was spreading in the islands. This, too, would dramatically alter the traditional world of Tawi-Tawi.

During all this activity, the population of Tawi-Tawi grew phenomenally. When I lived in the islands, the official census population was about 80,000; a recent official figure claimed 450,000 for the province. During my stay, Bongao's official population was approximately 5,000; a current estimate is 100,000 for the same municipality. When I first knew Bongao, it had one unpaved street, sporadic electricity, and an engine-less truck; now it has paved roads throughout the town and around the island, traffic jams, ATMs, TVs, an international airport, internet cafes, cell phones and all the other paraphernalia of contemporary urban life in the Philippines. Bridges connect some of the islands and the formerly uninhabited interior of Tawi-Tawi Island is rapidly becoming settled, mostly by Christians whose presence is not always welcomed by the indigenous Muslims. Massive environmental casualties have accompanied this growth, including reef destruction, water and air pollution, overfishing, forest depletion and beach removal.

Human casualties have also accompanied the change. Many Sama Dilaut were driven from the reefs that sustained their culture for centuries, some were killed in conflicts with newcomers and others fled for the relative security of nearby Sabah. Those who remained have abandoned their boat-dwelling life and are rapidly becoming incorporated into the Islamic culture of the land-dwelling Sama. The Sama Dilaut nomadic boat culture that I once knew no longer exists in Tawi-Tawi.

But that's another story for another writer.

ALSO BY H. ARLO NIMMO

The Sea People of Sulu

Bajau of the Philippines

The Pele Literature

The Songs of Salanda

Magosaha

The Andrews Sisters

Good and Bad Times in a San Francisco Neighborhood

Pele, Volcano Goddess of Hawaii